At the hea~ community

Community enterprise in a ch ᵥ world

John Pearce

Diagrams drawn by Alan Tuffs

Published by Calouste Gulbenkian Foundation, London 1993

John Pearce has been working in the field of Community Enterprise and Community Development for over 25 years in the UK and overseas. Until 1991 he was Chief Executive of Strathclyde Community Business which was the major support and financing organisation for community enterprises in the West of Scotland. He now runs his own consulting service, 'Community Enterprise Consultancy and Research'. In addition to advice and training for community enterprises he has developed a Community Futures process to engage a cross-section of community stakeholders in the local development process. His other interests include programme planning and project development, evaluation, social auditing and appropriate legal structures for community and social enterprises.

He has written extensively about community economic development and is involved with the community enterprise movement in Scotland, serving as a director of Community Business Scotland and as chair of the *New Sector* magazine. He is an active director with his local community business in West Calder and is chair of the Europe Section of the Commonwealth Association for Local Action and Economic Development (COMMACT).

Contents

Foreword

In the late 1970s the UK branch of the Calouste Gulbenkian Foundation extended its long-term support of community development in housing, environment, social welfare and other areas to local economic activity, or community enterprise. As well as funding action by local residents in response to unemployment, in 1980 the Foundation set up two national committees dealing with different aspects of community enterprise. One was established in collaboration with the Manpower Services Commission, and led to the influential report *Whose Business is Business?*, and the other, chaired by Lady Seear, proposed administrative and legislative changes to promote local economic activity. Subsequent years saw support for neighbourhood initiatives, training programmes, seminars, research, publications, and the building of infra-structure to encourage community enterprise at local, regional and national levels. Most recently we have been concerned with the potential for community enterprise in implementing community care and other contracted services.

During these years we shared the high expectations, misconceptions, disappointments and celebrations of success of those working in this field, referred to by John Pearce in this book. In it he has provided a valuable and highly readable historical perspective, setting the developments of the past 20 years or so in the context of the work of Robert Owen in the early 1800s, and that of the Rochdale Pioneers after 1844. As founder and former convenor of Community Business Scotland, and chief executive of Strathclyde Community Business Limited, and someone who since 1978 has worked closely with and influenced the Foundation's contribution to the development of community enterprise, we were pleased to back him in writing this thoughtful and creative book.

John Pearce takes a broad view of what should be considered to be community enterprises, and argues that they have a particular role to play in local development, being suited to providing services and running programmes which on the whole are neglected by the private sector and increasingly abandoned by the public sector. In terms of subsidiarity, the local community is a level to which a range of activities could be delegated, and community enterprise is a structure through which the local community can take effective action.

The outcome of community enterprise action cannot be measured effectively in traditional ways. John Pearce explores the need for a new system of auditing which assesses community profit, and describes one system which has been devised for community enterprises.

At the Heart of the Community Economy makes a strong case for understanding that the experience of community enterprises over the past two decades has demonstrated the relevance of the concept to local development problems in both urban and rural areas, but at the same time cautions against pretending that they are businesses like any other. In truth they are different and it is the difference that is important.

Paul Curno
Deputy Director
Calouste Gulbenkian Foundation, UK branch

Introduction

"This principle of individual interest, opposed as it is perpetually to the public good, is considered, by the most celebrated political economists, to be the cornerstone to the social system, and without which, society could not exist." [1]

This book is about the community economy and the community enterprises which make up an important part of it. Its focus is community enterprise in Britain.

Community enterprise is about local action in the community economy. But today as never before we must consider the local community within a much wider context. The problems which community enterprise activists are tackling in Britain are not unique to our country, they are the problems of a 'shrinking globe' where it is increasingly difficult to disentangle 'our' problems from 'their' problems. Poverty in Britain is part of a world phenomenon of growing poverty. Economic disempowerment afflicts the majority of the globe's inhabitants.

Community enterprises are distinctive because of their value base which puts people before profit, community benefit before return on investment: indeed their main purpose is to return community profit in a variety of forms. Their legal structures are open and accountable. They seek to be community-led partnerships, tackling economic, social and environmental issues in a holistic fashion.

In Britain community enterprise has emerged over the past two decades as a response to and as a consequence of the growth of poverty and disadvantage in our society. It is a grassroots movement of local people asking the question "what can we do?" and deciding that it is preferable to take action on their own account rather than wait for 'someone else' to come and do it for them; it is local communities seeking to obtain some power over their situation and their prospects. For the most part community enterprise has been considered a strategy particularly relevant to the poorest and most economically marginal areas and it is in those communities that the ideas of collective self-help have taken strongest root. However that should not imply that the idea of community enterprise is only an idea for the poor and the disadvantaged, for the marginal and the weak.

The following pages argue that community enterprise has a particular and valuable role to play in local development, being suited to providing services and running programmes which on the whole are neglected by the private sector and increasingly abandoned by the public sector. In terms of subsidiarity, the local community is the level to which a range of activities should be delegated and community enterprises the structure through which the local community can take effective action on its own behalf. It is furthermore argued that community enterprises are different and should be recognised as such, being granted effective legislative recognition and special assistance as *the* way to achieve local development.

Community enterprise is about local communities 'doing' rather than 'being done to': empowerment is the currently fashionable word. It is the "act local" of Gandhi's dictum. In the 'global village' of the 1990s the poor and the dispossessed face similar problems wherever they are. Local action in Britain is mirrored by local action around the globe and that action aims, eventually, to change the way things are, to ensure that development is people-centred and sustainable.

The outcomes of such action cannot be measured effectively in traditional ways. We need a new system of auditing, of assessing community profit; a system which can be credible to help persuade a fast-changing world of the need to adopt and to adapt to new ways.

Community enterprise has struggled and flourished in Britain over the past two decades, reviving ideas which echo from the past and placing them into a twentieth century reality. I am truly grateful to the Calouste Gulbenkian Foundation for giving me the opportunity of reflecting on these matters and discussing them with a number of people who have been involved in different ways with the community enterprise movement in Britain. Their names are listed in an appendix and they can be seen broadly to represent four categories: local activists or managers from a particular community enterprise; persons who have developed and/or run support programmes for community enterprises; representatives of resourcing regimes for community enterprise; and known 'thinkers' about community enterprise and the local economy.

All have given generously and enthusiastically of their time and I have been struck by the strength of common ground that exists, especially as regards the important role community enterprises should be able to play within the community economy and as regards the essential moral force of the community enterprise idea. Their ideas, comments and analysis have all influenced the content and direction of the following pages but ultimately the responsibility for what is written is entirely mine and I make no claim in any way to represent the views of others.

I am especially grateful to Joanna Pearce, Colin Roxburgh, Peter Smith and Alan Tuffs who read and commented on the first draft, to Ken Alexander who tackled the second draft and to Stephen Phillips who advised on chapter 11. Additional thanks are also due to Alan Tuffs who has drawn the diagrams which we hope illuminate the words. Finally I must thank Paul Curno of the Gulbenkian Foundation for his forbearance, his guidance and his support during the project.

Chapters 1 and 2 set the context, starting with a brief description of community enterprise in Britain in 1992 and an examination of the historical traditions from the nineteenth century. A separate essay in the appendices describes the global context of poverty, ecological threat and human disempowerment within which community enterprise world-wide attempts to exert some modifying influence.

Chapter 3 examines the all-important value base which distinguishes community enterprise from other forms of business and development, and describes the community enterprise model both in theory and in action.

Chapter 4 analyses the sorts of activities which community enterprises have shown themselves to be good at: activities which "touch the life of the neighbourhood". It is suggested that it is possible to define a community economy within which community enterprises might be the main form of enterprise organisation.

Chapter 5 explores the nature of community, touching on issues of scale and viability and localness, while chapter 6 discusses the all-important human capital on which community enterprise depends for success - or failure. Chapter 7 examines ways in which community enterprises can ensure that they are accountable to the communities which have created them and which they are designed to benefit.

Chapters 8 and 9 look at relations with the public and the private sectors. Sometimes community enterprise is represented as a threat or as an irrelevance; but real local progress and success will seldom be achieved except where local communities can work in equal partnership with private companies and with the public sector agencies.

Chapter 10 discusses some of the problems associated with introducing private investment into community enterprises and describes recent social investment initiatives. Chapter 11 presents the argument in favour of special legislative recognition and chapter 12 emphasises the need to measure both the 'soft' and the 'hard' outcomes of community enterprise. A model process is described.

The concluding chapter 13 summarises some of the important issues which face the community enterprise movement in Britain and society's reaction to it and offers some pointers for action which could lead to intentional and substantial growth of the community enterprise sector in the twenty-first century.

Simply put, community enterprise is a practical way of using business to regenerate the local community, to deliver local services and to tackle social problems. It is about development that benefits people. It is an idea which is not new, nor is it especially British: community enterprise is being developed all over the globe in rich countries and in poor, in North and South. It is a part of a world-wide movement to embrace the concept of people-centred development and to follow Gandhi in thinking global while acting local.

John Pearce
Community Enterprise Consultancy and Research
Harburn

Chapter 1

Community enterprise in Britain 1992

"To effect any permanently beneficial change in society, I found it was far more necessary to act than to speak."

Community Enterprise is a generic term which is used to include a range of enterprising and business activities which operate within and as part of the community economy. They are variously referred to as community businesses, community co-operatives, development trusts, community development corporations. A booklet recently published in the north of Scotland uses the term 'community trading organisation' [1] to distinguish community-based organisations which trade from those which do not. It is however a distinction which gets less clear the closer the community economy is examined with its voluntary input and its positioning at the interface between the informal and the formal economies.

It is a distinctive value base which very clearly distinguishes community enterprise both from private business and from public enterprise. That value base is to do with community roots,[2] community accountability, community benefit and community ownership of wealth and of assets.

The community enterprise sector may be divided into three sub-sectors according to type of activity: 1. business or trading; 2. housing; and 3. finance. The housing sub-sector comprises community-based housing associations, housing co-operatives and tenant management co-operatives and the finance sub-sector credit unions and a handful of specialist financial organisations. The business or trading sub-sector is the most diverse collection of initiatives and is the main focus of attention for this book. Taken together these three sub-sectors represent a powerful economic force and also a powerful human force involving as they do substantial numbers of local people as activists in the shaping and running of their local community economy.

1. The business or trading sub-sector

North Kensington Amenity Trust

The 1991 Community Enterprise Award Scheme run by *The Times* newspaper in association with the Royal Institute of British Architects (RIBA) and Business in the Community (BITC) introduced a new 'sustainability' award for a project that has made a significant and continuing development contribution to its local community for at least 20 years. The first winner was the North Kensington Amenity Trust (NKAT) formed as a result of the anguish and anger of local residents at the consequences to their local community of driving the elevated section of the M40 from Westbourne Park to White City. A swathe of North Kensington was bulldozed and street communities literally cut in half. And on completion of the motorway, traffic swept into London at first floor level while underneath was left a derelict concrete jungle of no-man's-land.

The Trust fought for and won the task of developing the 23 acres underneath the motorway and by 1992 all but three of those acres had been developed: one-fifth for commercial use and four-fifths for community use. The commercial developments, which include shops, offices, light industrial workshops and an outdoor market, make a significant contribution to the local economy and fund the Trust's administrative and development work. Community usage includes open space and urban parkland, football pitches, a sports centre, a fitness and snooker centre and office space for local and city charities. The 170 tenants of the Trust provide over 750 local jobs.

Described as a "partnership between community groups and the local authority to repair the damage"[3] the Trust is now a financially self-supporting body with an annual turnover above £1m and assets estimated to exceed £20m. It has an annual budget of £65,000 to provide small grants to local community organisations.

NKAT is a product of 1960s style community action (the Westway was built during the 1960s and opened by Michael Heseltine in July 1970) and was born out of the anger of local people about how their homes and community had been disregarded in the rush to build the urban motorway. When it was opened the first floor front rooms of Acklam Road were a mere 20 feet from six lanes of speeding motorway traffic! Early years of conflict with 'authority' have now been replaced by what is described as "productive tension" in a book celebrating the Trust's 21st birthday, the Trust working with the public and private sectors for the benefit of the community "not hidebound like a public authority nor as strongly entrepreneurial as the private sector".[4] Its independence is seen as important and its strength is based on solid financial assets: "Its flexibility has broadened on the back of its growing financial strength, allowing it to meet changing community needs. New roles and a larger vision can grow from its established base. The ability to accommodate a wide range of constituencies in its community has meant no single interest group controls the Trust".[5]

Coin Street Community Builders

Coin Street Community Builders is another community enterprise with its roots in the community action tradition of the 1960s and early 1970s: "Narrow definitions of 'what was wrong' (my roof leaks) gave way to wider perspectives (we are losing all our supermarkets), to explanations (because of the loss of the local population) and to solutions (we need more family housing built in the area)".[6]

Coin Street is a 13-acre site in the heart of London's Waterloo on the South Bank, next to the National Theatre and including the highly distinctive Oxo building. It was a part of London which was rapidly being given over to office and hotel developments until the Waterloo Community Development Group, later Coin Street Action Group, called for "homes not offices" to redress the balance and mix of uses in the area.

A first public inquiry rejected both the office/hotel proposal to build Europe's tallest skyscraper put forward by a commercial developer and the community's alternative plan to concentrate on low cost housing for local people and community facilities. The developers' plans were criticised as "massive and over-dominant" and the community schemes as "failing to exploit the employment potential of the sites".[7] At a second public inquiry in 1983 direct community action in the shape of 400 local people plus press and television were needed to defer the inquiry until after the GLC elections and to prevent the outgoing (conservative) administration from selling off its part of the Coin Street site to the office developers even before their scheme gained approval.

In the event the GLC changed hands and the inquiry inspector gave permission to go ahead for either the office development or the revised community scheme, which now included proposals for managed workspace and a shopping area. Active help from the GLC and both Borough Councils (Lambeth and Southwark include part of Coin

Street) and sustained community pressure led to the office developers pulling out and by July 1984 the entire site had been sold to a community enterprise company set up by local community groups: Coin Street Community Builders Ltd.

In the short-term the site was used for car-parking giving the community enterprise an income to service its capital debt and also the revenue to sustain its administration and development work. Within four years the first housing co-operative had been built and occupied; a new park and river walk were opened. Other housing developments have now taken place and eventually there will be homes for some 1,300 people. Gabriel's Wharf is a 'workspace street' adjacent to the Thames accommodating restaurants, food shops, craft and clothing manufacturers and retailers. Eventually the Oxo building will incorporate more craft and other workshops, cafes and restaurants, a Thames museum, exhibition and performance areas and additional housing.

The Coin Street slogan "There is another way" proclaims that city centre development can be done for the benefit of the local community, can be controlled by local people and can be financially viable.

The Loftus Development Trust

In rural East Cleveland (formerly North Yorkshire) the Loftus Development Trust (LDT) has been created as a result of an initiative undertaken by the Civic Trust Regeneration Unit working with local residents to create a local development organisation. Loftus is a small town which was once the centre of an iron-ore extractive industry. The LDT has given local people the chance to decide for themselves what local development priorities should be. A playground has been built in a council housing estate, the former council house has been converted into a small high quality workspace, a derelict cinema and adjacent site is being developed to provide housing behind and shops fronting onto the main street, an environmental improvement programme has been agreed for the old market square.

North Kensington, Coin Street and Loftus are all examples of community enterprises which call themselves development trusts. For the most part development trusts are located in England and their primary concerns are for property and environmental development, but they also become involved in other forms of social and economic action. In February 1992 a conference was held in Birmingham to

A Glossary Bookmark for
At the heart of the community economy
by John Pearce

ABCUL	Association of British Credit Unions Ltd
ACEHI	Association of Community Enterprises in the Highlands and Islands
APT	Area for Priority Treatment
ARC	Action Resource Centre
ASDO	Association of Scottish Development Organisations
BACEN	Bristol and Avon Community Enterprise Network
BITC	Business in the Community
CBS	Community Business Scotland
CCI	Corporate Community Involvement
CCT	Compulsory Competitive Tendering
CDC	Community Development Corporation
CEP	Community Enterprise Programme
CE-UK	Community Enterprise UK
COMMACT	Commonwealth Association for Local Action and Economic Development
CP	Community Programme
DOE	Department of the Environment
DTA	Development Trusts Association
EA	Employment Action
EC	European Commission/Community
ECOP	Employee Common Ownership Plan
ERDF	European Regional Development Fund
ESF	European Social Fund
ESOP	Employee Share Ownership Plan
ET	Employment Training
GLC	Greater London Council
GWL	Govan Workspace Ltd
HIDB	Highlands and Islands Development Board
HIE	Highlands and Islands Enterprise
ICO	Industrial Common Ownership
ICOF	Industrial Common Ownership Finance Ltd
ICOM	Industrial Common Ownership Movement Ltd
JCP	Job Creation Programme
LDT	Loftus Development Trust
LEA	Local Enterprise Agency
LEC	Local Enterprise Company
LEAP	Local Enterprise Advisory Project
MBA	Master of Business Administration
NKAT	North Kensington Amenity Trust
PFA	People for Action
RIBA	Royal Institute of British Architects
SCBL	Strathclyde Community Business Ltd
SCEIF	Scottish Community Enterprise Investment Fund plc
STEP	Special Temporary Employment Programme
SSHA	Scottish Special Housing Association
SURE	Shape Urban Renewal Enterprises Ltd
TEC	Training and Enterprise Council

consider the formation of a Development Trusts Association (DTA) and the Association was subsequently launched in April in London. Research carried out as part of the feasibility study for the Association identified a total of 647 organisations which either are or might in part be doing work as a development trust.[8] During the summer of 1992 the Department of the Environment approved a core funding grant to permit the Association to establish a London headquarters with a small staff, the post of director being advertised in the national press in September. The consequence of DOE funding is effectively to make the DTA an English organisation.[9] Plans have therefore been developed to set up a Scottish equivalent, the Association of Scottish Development Organisations (ASDO), which was launched at a meeting held in West Calder in October 1992.

Community enterprise in Scotland

In Scotland the modern history of the business and trading sub-sector of community enterprise dates from 1977 when the Highlands and Islands Development Board (HIDB) launched their community co-operative scheme. Targeted initially at the Western Isles where unemployment had been historically high and where imaginative use had been made of the Job Creation Programme introduced by the Manpower Services Commission in 1975, the HIDB scheme was a public sector intervention to stimulate community-based economic activity, inspired by the then chairman of the HIDB, Sir Kenneth Alexander, and drawing on the experience of communities in the Gaeltacht of Ireland.

The HIDB scheme provided for field workers to promote the idea of community enterprise amongst local communities[10] and to guide and support local steering committees once formed. The scheme also offered matching grant-aid for initial capital raised locally, grants to finance the early appointment of a manager and access to the usual HIDB package of financial assistance for small businesses. The HIDB produced a set of model community co-operative rules which were approved by the Registrar of Friendly Societies. The community co-operative support package proved successful in the Western Isles and was soon extended to cover the whole of the HIDB area. It also served as the basic model, bringing together field work stimulation and support, management grant, access to capital and a model constitution, on which has been based the community enterprise support network established in most Scottish regions[11] funded through local and central government and which has now begun to spread into England.

Outwith the Highlands and Islands it was in Strathclyde Region that the first support structure for community enterprise, the Local Enterprise Advisory Project (LEAP) was set up in 1978 as a small urban aid voluntary project based within the Local Government Unit of Paisley College.[12] LEAP worked with other community development activists in central Scotland to develop the idea of the community company, similar to the community co-operative but using company legislation: a multi-functional trading organisation to create viable employment, provide local services, offer training opportunities and act as a focus for local development. The community company idea caught the imagination of many local people and their organisations in areas of high unemployment who wanted to get on and do something rather than wait for someone else to do 'it'. The first community company to start trading was Craigmillar Festival Enterprises Ltd in Edinburgh in 1979[13] and by 1980 three more had been registered and were trading in Strathclyde. A national federation, the Scottish Community Enterprise Forum (later to become Community Business Scotland) was formed.

The national organisation was to play an important part in giving the idea of the community company an identity and a collective sense of movement, campaigning, publishing a newsletter and lobbying for political and financial support. A combination of grassroots momentum, the active support of key local authority members and officials and the willing use of the urban programme by the Scottish Office led to rapid community enterprise growth, first in the west of Scotland (Strathclyde Region) and later in the other regions. By 1984 a dedicated community enterprise support organisation was created in Strathclyde, Strathclyde Community Business Ltd (SCBL), providing field work promotion and support, business development advice, training, and financial investment both grant-aid and loans, the bulk of the investment finance coming from the urban programme and thus directed at the 'areas for priority treatment'.[14]

SCBL was created as an 'arm's-length' company, independent of the public sector but almost totally dependent on the public sector for its funding. This pattern of structure and remit served as the pattern for support organisations set up in the other regions of Scotland with the exception of the Highlands and Islands. There the support task was transferred in 1985 from the HIDB to the Association of Community Enterprises in the Highlands and Islands (ACEHI), a federation made up of the community enterprises in the area. Two district councils within Strathclyde have also since set up their own small community enterprise development units.[15]

A consequence of the support network and the positive backing of the public sector was a rapid growth in community enterprise during the middle 1980s throughout Scotland. There have been some notable successes, and some failures too.

Papay Community Co-operative

Papa Westray is a small island community of some 80 inhabitants in the far north of the Orkney archipelago. Through the Papay Community Co-operative the islanders run their own general store and the only hotel on the island with its associated youth hostel. They also have a range of self-catering accommodation and have published a number of tourist booklets. Papa Westray is famous for its bird-watching and for the oldest known human house in Europe, the Knap of Howar.

It is perfectly reasonable to claim that the enterprise of the community co-operative has been a significant factor in stemming depopulation and increasing the tourist trade, thus helping to keep the island community viable.

Govan Workspace

In urban Glasgow Govan Workspace Ltd (GWL) pioneered the managed workspace concept in Scotland by converting a former primary school - contrary to all the pundits' predictions - into a successful work-creating project. GWL had grown out of a European-funded anti-poverty project where local residents had quickly fastened onto the fundamental problem of rising local unemployment and a declining local economy and decided they, as local people, wanted to do something about it. The workspace idea was then in its infancy in England and was unknown in Scotland. They determined to introduce it north of the border, confident that the idea of small workshops on an easy-in easy-out lease basis with common services and advice and help to hand could play an important part in encouraging new businesses to set up in their part of the city.

By 1992 the company owned three sites in Govan: the former primary school, a former Lyons bakery and the former shipyard apprentice training school, together providing some 120 workshops and work for over 450 people. The company also runs a workspace cafe and outside catering business and is a provider of training for potential entrepreneurs and for unemployed people trying to return to the labour market.

Govan Workspace has become a successful business but not without the struggle so often needed when a community-based group wishes to do something not usually associated with community action, as Buchanan pointed out in his study of the early history of Govan Workspace: "It is a remarkable success story, but not one without problems which continue even now. It is a story which demonstrates great determination and persistence on the part of a dedicated group of local people who were intent on doing something constructive in their local economy and who simply would not take 'No' for an answer. It is a story which shows public agencies uncertain and cautious in dealing with a community group wanting to get involved in a commercial activity and property management. It is a story in which a new and innovative concept has now become widely accepted".[16]

The Allander Group

In the pre-war housing estate of Possil, one mile north of Glasgow's city centre, the community enterprise, the Allander Group, has become the biggest 'private' employer in the locality. The enterprise runs four successful divisions employing over 120 people: security, cleaning, painting and decorating, and landscaping. Allander Security was one of the pioneers of the neighbourhood security contracts in Glasgow providing 24 hour patrols in some of the most at-risk estates in the city to ensure that void houses and other public property was not damaged. The results were remarkably successful not only ensuring that the housing escaped vandalism but generally making the areas safer and capable of improvement. Recently some of these security contracts have been expanded to include elements of estate caretaking: de-littering, cleaning void houses, cleaning closes and stairs, reporting broken lights, gas leaks, plumbing problems and other defects to ensure speedy action. Informally the security/caretaking staff keep an eye on the local housebound and the elderly, gather used syringes, and provide emergency contact with the outside world during night-time hours. Local people doing local work and keeping their own community running more smoothly.

The community enterprise plays an active part in local affairs and even sponsors the local football team: Glasgow Perthshire. The enterprise is profitable with an annual turnover in the region of £1.25m and is able now to finance development initiatives from its reserves.

Barrowfield Community Business

Along with successes there have been failures. Indeed one of the community enterprise lessons that British bureaucracy has found hardest to learn is that in order to have success you must both risk and inevitably experience failure.

One of the best known community enterprises to have gone into liquidation was Barrowfield Community Business in Glasgow's east end. Barrowfield had pioneered neighbourhood security along with Possil. It was in Barrowfield that landscaping and environmental work done by local people transformed the appearance of the area and demonstrated that if local people do local work it is more likely to be valued and to last. It was in Barrowfield that a local authority tenement block of flats was converted into an office/light industrial workspace managed by the community business. The company ran a large Community Programme Managing Agency which was able to get local long-term unemployed people back into work, often moving on from their CP work into the wider labour market. At its peak the community enterprise employed circa 100 people in its commercial projects and over 150 in its CP and training projects.

The community enterprise played a key role in a web of local community activities and initiatives which made a very visible impact on the appearance of the estate and on the quality of life for local residents, especially apparent to those who had known the area previously as one of the city's most difficult, deprived and depressed localities. Barrowfield probably received more visitors from all over the world than any other Scottish community enterprise, including two of Mrs Thatcher's 'think tankers',[17] who came to see how local people doing local work and in active partnership with the local authority, the Scottish Development Agency and several private sector companies could begin to transform their community and their lives.

The enterprise ran into a number of problems. There were continuing management problems; it proved virtually impossible to find the 'right' person to manage the complex organisation. The enterprise overstretched itself - often encouraged by public and private sector agencies equally caught up in the exciting momentum of action - in terms of the number of projects and businesses it became involved in. Financial controls did not show soon enough that the landscaping contracts were making losses. Political attitudes in Glasgow at the time of the changeover from the Community Programme to Employment Training forced the company to give up its managing agency and with it an important annual profit contribution towards general costs. Confusion over a matching public sector grant for a training scheme led to claims for the immediate repayment of a loan. All these factors combined to bring the company to the point of insolvency.

The insolvency practitioner who examined the situation recommended that circa £100,000 be injected into the community enterprise in order to keep it going because of the social value of its work and the social dis-benefit which closure would occasion. This course of action was also advocated by the staff of the regional support organisation, Strathclyde Community Business Limited (SCBL), who believed that the necessary management improvements could be brought about and that the past energy and commitment of the people of Barrowfield deserved continuing support. This was not to condone poor management and financial practices but to recognise the complex nature of the problems facing the enterprise, not all of which were of their own making.

It turned out that the two local authority sponsors who were the only possible lifelines for the Barrowfield Community Enterprise decided that they could only judge the matter on business support criteria. And on business support criteria alone the enterprise had failed. New investment was refused and the enterprise, including all its subsidiaries, was forced to go into liquidation. Much of what had been built up was lost, although the security jobs were saved through Allander Security taking over the contract. The closure of Barrowfield was to have considerable repercussions throughout the community enterprise world and brought into sharp focus key questions about which criteria should be used by which to judge success and failure.

Community Business Scotland

By the time of the 1992 annual convention of Community Business Scotland (CBS) it was estimated that there were some 170 community enterprises established and trading in Scotland which together support some 3,300 jobs and training places, excluding jobs created by the tenants of community enterprise run workspaces. The collective turnover of these enterprises in 1992 was estimated to be £18m.

As the national federation in Scotland, CBS has played a key role in the development of the sector. It has given a focus, provided an important networking function and has pressed and lobbied strongly for support of the community enterprise idea and, during the 1980s, for the creation of the regional support organisations. CBS had published the *CB News*, 44 issues from December 1981 to December 1991, when it was succeeded by the *New Sector* magazine, a joint venture with the Industrial Common Ownership Movement[18] and Community Enterprise UK (CE-UK). CBS runs an annual convention which has served as the main national community enterprise conference and meeting ground, each year attracting as many as 30% of its participants from south of the border. Its Legal Structures Working Party has monitored the model legal structures and in 1991/2 published a revised and updated version.[19] In addition to being a campaigning, lobbying and networking organisation, CBS runs a range of training and information seminars and workshops. The CBS group includes the Scottish Community Enterprise Investment Fund plc.

In 1991 Scottish Enterprise (formerly the Scottish Development Agency) recognised the potentially important role of a national organisation and offered a core funding grant. This has allowed the organisation to appoint, for the first time, a full-time director and gives the opportunity to build up an expanded programme of services for its members and for the regional support organisations.

Community Enterprise UK

CE-UK was established in 1988 as a UK body to link the growing community enterprise network and to promote the concept in England and Wales. Because of the already strong and well-established structures in Scotland, CE-UK has effectively been an English/Welsh organisation directing its energies to community enterprise growth south of the border. CBS is represented on its board.

There is no common pattern of support for community enterprise in England or Wales and there is great regional diversity in development and support arrangements. The greatest concentrations of activity appear to be in the north-east and the midlands although a lack of basic collected information about what is happening on the ground makes firm statements impossible. CE-UK estimates that there might be as many as 275 community enterprises established in England, but until a basic 'mapping' exercise has been done no one knows how many business and trading community enterprises exist. Nor is it clear what the overlap is between CE-UK numbers and the DTA database.[20]

In some areas the lead has been taken by the voluntary sector as in Birmingham where Co-Enterprise operates as a community enterprise support organisation for the city or in Salford where an organisation called Start-up operates. Elsewhere the local authority has taken the lead and appointed an officer dedicated to community enterprise work, as in Middlesbrough and in Leicester City where the council has appointed four specialist officers. A more recent example is a joint initiative between the local authority and the private sector to fund the Bristol and Avon Community Enterprise Network (BACEN).[21]

In Wales the central government quango, the Welsh Development Agency, has established a small in-house community enterprise unit. A directory of community enterprise contacts produced in 1992 lists 54 community businesses either trading or at the planning stage and seven local specialist community enterprise support agencies. Community Enterprise Wales acts as a networking federation.

2. The housing sub-sector

It is the housing sub-sector of community enterprise which is the longest established, having been part of the local development and regeneration scene since the early 1970s. Community-based housing associations have played a key role - particularly in the city of Glasgow - in regenerating inner-city neighbourhoods by refurbishing older properties and providing well-managed affordable social housing. Their localness - often to very small neighbourhoods - has encouraged a high level of community participation in management and in organising social activities for members and tenants. Over time these housing associations have begun to play a greater part in local development: building new houses and looking to become involved in other forms of activity, in particular community care and economic and employment development.

The Queens Cross Housing Association in Glasgow was one of the first to act, setting up a sister company, Queens Cross Workspace Ltd, to develop and manage small workshops for local new start small businesses. The Central Govan Housing Association, the first community-based association to be set up in Glasgow, has its own architectural practice which works for other clients as well as for the association. The Langridge Crescent Housing Co-operative in Middlesbrough has recently opened an Initiative Centre to act as a focus for local development. Facilities include small workshops, training facilities, administrative services, community shop, cafe and launderette, meeting rooms and a playgroup. The Liverpool Eldonians, in addition to having built the biggest housing co-operative in Europe, have become involved through their Development Trust in training programmes for young unemployed and in a range of business ventures: a garden centre (run in partnership with a private businessman), a children's nursery (a joint venture with Littlewoods) and an old persons home (a joint venture with a specialist housing association).

In the Scottish borders the Waverley Housing Trust has taken housing which formerly belonged to the Scottish Special Housing Association[22] into community ownership and through its related management company provides high quality, tenant sensitive housing management and at the same time is creating local jobs not only in housing administration but also in repair and maintenance work and in environmental work.

The SHAPE group in Birmingham comprises Shape Housing Association Ltd and a subsidiary company Shape Urban Renewal Enterprises Ltd (SURE). It calls itself "one of Britain's more unusual housing association groups involved in a wide range of neighbourhood-based projects - employment, environment, training and neighbourhood development".[23] It runs hostels, has its own architectural practice, runs a managed workspace and operates a number of 'training businesses': builders, garage services, metal work and a market garden. They also offer community workshop and business start-up assistance in their 'Access Centre'. Together with the South London Family Housing Association, Shape has launched a new initiative called People for Action (PFA) aimed to link investment in social housing with local and economic development and to encourage housing organisations to play a more active part in other aspects of development, building on their human as well as their business experience.

The Housing Association movement has a very strong organisation throughout Britain, reflecting the important role which the voluntary housing movement has developed since the nineteenth century. The National Federation of Housing Associations which serves England was founded in 1935 and has ten regional offices. It publishes a weekly paper (*Housing Associations Weekly*) and a monthly magazine (*Voluntary Housing*). The Scottish Federation of Housing Associations, which includes the Confederation of Scottish Housing Co-operatives, has three regional offices and publishes its own monthly magazine (*Federation Focus*). The monthly magazine of the *Welsh Federation* is called *Cartref*.

The Federations all provide a comprehensive information and advice service both for existing voluntary housing organisations and groups considering establishing one. The Federations give the voluntary housing movement a strong identity and the ability to act together to influence policy, conduct research and lobby government and other bodies as appropriate. Small community-based housing organisations are more common in Scotland than elsewhere and there are real fears within the movement that national policy and funding arrangements might threaten the continued existence of these smaller, local associations.

3. Finance sub-sector

The finance sub-sector of community enterprise mainly comprises the credit unions which offer people the opportunity to save regularly and to obtain loans at affordable rates of interest. The number of credit unions in Britain, especially those which are community-based, has been growing rapidly in recent years, not least because of the appointment of development officers by local authorities, often using urban programme funding. This growth has been in local communities especially where the establishment of a credit union is seen as a positive step in combating the power of the 'loan sharks'. It is now estimated that there are 300 community-based credit unions in Britain. Most except the very biggest are run entirely by local volunteers who contribute significant amounts of time to handling the quite detailed administration which is involved.

There are two national credit union bodies: the National Federation which specialises in community-based credit unions and the Association of British Credit Unions Ltd (ABCUL) which deals both with community-based unions and with workplace or industry-based unions.

Within the community economy credit unions play the important role of providing affordable credit and encouraging saving. This could be the foundation of a future community banking system with local deposits being used for local development rather than becoming lost in the national and international financial systems.[24]

There also exist certain funding organisations which channel finance into community enterprises and which may also be considered as part of the finance sub-sector of community enterprise. The one dedicated fund so far established is the Scottish Community Enterprise Investment Fund plc (SCEIF) which raised a preference share capital of circa £250,000 in 1989 for investment in Scottish community enterprises. A considerable part of the investment portfolio of Mercury

Provident plc consists of community enterprises of one sort or another and discussions between SCEIF and Mercury have explored how the latter might target more of its investment at community enterprises. Mercury is essentially an 'alternative bank' which offers its depositors the opportunity to support socially valuable initiatives. This is 'social investment': the notion that money should be used not only to obtain a financial reward, but also to produce a benefit for the planet or its people, or both.

Consequent upon the reorganisation of the support arrangements for community enterprise in Scotland's Strathclyde Region the financing role is now the specific task of a separate company, Community Investment in Strathclyde, rather than one of the tasks of a multi-purpose support organisation. This model is likely to be followed in other areas and will thus increase the number of financial organisations dedicated to investing in community enterprise.

The overall picture

The picture which emerges is of a considerable and growing sector of activity. The full extent is not known as it has not been fully 'mapped' and there are almost certainly organisations, projects and enterprises which are effectively community enterprises by what they do and how they are structured, but do not recognise themselves as such.

If the amount of economic activity, the assets, the numbers of people involved were aggregated for community enterprises of all types, the numbers would be large: a significant body of experience, a significant part of the community economy, and a significant force for change. An important question facing the sector is how the individual parts can work together to press for change while retaining individuality and accountability to their varied local communities.

Chapter 2

An historical perspective

"It is well known that a combination of men and interests can effect that which it would be futile to attempt, and impossible to accomplish, by individual exertions and separate interests. Then why, it may be inquired, have men so long acted individually, and in opposition to each other?"

Pioneering in Rochdale

On the evening of 21st December 1844 the shutters were taken down from a new shop on the ground floor of a warehouse at 31 Toad Lane, Rochdale. The opening stock had cost £16 11s 11d and consisted of 28lb butter, 56lb sugar, 6cwt flour, a sack of oatmeal and some tallow candles. The Rochdale Society of Equitable Pioneers had started to trade.

To start with, the shop opened on Saturday and Monday evenings only but by March 1845 it was opening on every weekday evening except Tuesday. By the end of the first year of trading it had a membership of 74, had turned over £781 and made a profit of £22.

Five years later by 1850 membership had increased to 600, trading turnover to £13,180 and profits to £991. Drapery, tailoring, butchery and footwear sections had been added to the general provisions and in 1851 the store was opened during the day-time like a regular shop. A newsroom and a library was also provided for members and customers.

It was the gradual but definite success of the Pioneers' Society which has been credited with the foundation of what since became the Co-operative Movement. Their model was copied by others and by 1851 it is estimated that there were at least 130 societies running co-operative stores across the country. In 1850 the Pioneers joined with a nearby co-operative store (the Brickfield Equitable Pioneers Society) to form a corn milling society which was the first successful joint venture between retail societies. By the end of 1852, eight years after the Toad Lane store first opened, 22 local retail societies were dealing with the corn mill and joining it as members.

A Rochdale Co-operative Manufacturing Society was also established based on the 'bounty to labour' principle of workers sharing in the profits. The success of the venture led to the need for a new and larger mill for which capital had to be raised. New share-holders who subscribed did not however share the same commitment as the founders to the profit-sharing principle and by 1862 they had been able to overturn the bounty to labour policy and practice. Thus the company became no different from any other business, making profits for its share-holders only. This experience has had a profound influence, which persists to the present day, on co-operative concerns about the potential power and influence of external shareholdings. William Cooper, one of the Rochdale pioneers who was involved with the manufacturing society, explained the basic issue at the time: "Nearly all the anti-bountyites are persons who joined the Society after it had become a prosperous and paying establishment...It appears to me wrong for persons to enter a Society with whose principles they disagree, and then destroy its constitution".[1]

The Pioneers became involved in other societies: the Equitable Provident Sick and Burial Society, the Co-operative Card Manufacturing Society, a Co-operative Building Society and the Co-operative Insurance Society. During the 1850s the Rochdale Society acted as a wholesaler for other nearby stores and then in 1863 played a leading role in the formation of the Co-operative Wholesale Society.

Education was an important objective for the early co-operative movement and the Rochdale Pioneers used their premises for lectures and discussions and early on established a library and reading room. After the passage of the Industrial and Provident Societies Act in 1853 it was permissible to devote 2.5% of profits to educational purposes. An education committee was formed and by 1855 the Society was organising school lessons for young people as well as adult education. This educational objective was considered of great importance "for the Society regarded its members not as customers but as co-operators whose minds, as well as their stomachs, required nourishment".[2]

The Rochdale Society was set up during the 'hungry forties', a time of poverty, hunger and social unrest. Many of the founding Pioneers were weavers, a group badly hit by the economic and social problems of the time, but Arnold Bonner in his classic book *British Co-operation*[3] is quick to point out that not all the founders were poor, that a number were relatively well-off artisans and that it was "Idealism, the vision of a better social order, not hunger (which) inspired these men". That idealism, that search for a better way is clearly stated in the objectives of the Society which were set down in their rules (**figure i**).

The objects of the Society were stated in "Law the First" of their rules as follows:-

The objects and plans of this Society are to form arrangements for the pecuniary benefit, and improvement of the social and domestic condition of its members, by raising a sufficient amount of capital in shares of one pound each, to bring into operation the following plans and arrangements.

The establishment of a store for the sale of provisions, clothing etc.

The building, purchasing or erecting of a number of houses, in which those members desiring to assist each other in improving their domestic and social condition may reside.

To commence the manufacture of such articles as the Society may determine upon, for the employment of such members as may be without employment or who may be suffering in consequence of repeated reductions in their wages.

As a further benefit and security to the members of this Society, the Society shall purchase or rent an estate or estates of land, which shall be cultivated by the members who may be out of employment, or whose labour may be badly remunerated.

That as soon as practicable the Society shall proceed to arrange the powers of production, distribution, education and government, or in other words, to establish a self-supporting home colony of united interests, or assist other societies in establishing such colonies.

That for the promotion of sobriety, a temperance hotel be opened in one of the Society's houses as soon as convenient.

Figure i Objects of the Rochdale Pioneers

The creation of a store was to be but the first step towards a much bigger vision of establishing a co-operative community. Bonner explains: "...the Pioneers commenced business with the purpose of pioneering the way to a new and better social order. Without that ideal the Society would never have begun; without it the difficulties of the early years would not have been overcome, the efforts to promote and assist other societies never have been made, and the developments which created national organisations never thought of".

Co-operative activity before Rochdale

Although Rochdale is considered to have been the start of the British Co-operative Movement, in fact there had been considerable co-operative activity throughout the 1830s based on the thinking and ideas of Robert Owen, as developed by early co-operative thinkers and practitioners such as Dr William King in Brighton who published *The Co-operator* between 1828 and 1830, and Alexander Campbell in Scotland who claimed to have been advocating co-operative principles and practice as early as 1818, and to have helped set up a co-operative baking society in Glasgow in 1822.

Two co-operative societies were formed in Brighton in 1827: the Brighton Co-operative Benevolent Association and the Co-operative Trading Association. By the end of 1828 Dr King knew of nine trading co-operative stores and by 1830 he claimed that more than 300 had been established throughout the country. A first Co-operative Congress was held in Manchester in 1831 and there was an annual congress until 1835, by when this first phase of co-operative experiment had virtually collapsed although some individual societies survived until after 1844 and then became part of the re-started and successful movement.

Robert Owen

Robert Owen was born in Newtown, Montgomeryshire in 1771 and by the age of 10 he had started on his business career, first in a draper's shop in Lincolnshire and later in London where he learned both about the cloth trade and about making profits. By the age of 17 he was in Manchester, quickly acquiring spinning machines of his own, becoming the manager of a mill employing 500 people and then becoming the partner of the mill-owner. By 1800 he had moved to New Lanark on the River Clyde, married the daughter of the founder, David Dale, of the New Lanark mills and taken over the running of the mills.

Within 12 years Owen was not only running a highly successful and profitable business employing 2,000 people but New Lanark was attracting considerable attention for its 'new approach' to management. This approach was based on providing better living and working conditions for the labour-force and on providing education. He sought to reduce the hours of work and to raise the age at which children started work. He improved the housing in the village, provided a village store and medical care, and set up a sick fund. He built a school for the village children - the Institute for the Formation of Character - which opened in 1816.

His system was paternalistic and very disciplined. Cleanliness was enforced. People found drunk in public were fined. He introduced the 'silent monitor', a block of wood displayed next to each person's workstation and with four coloured sides: white, yellow, blue and black. Each day the monitor was set by the departmental superintendent to record not only work performance, but also general behaviour - the 'character' of the person which Owen believed was formed by the environment in which they lived and worked. In his autobiography he records: "At the commencement of this new method of recording character, the great majority were black, many blue and a few yellow: gradually the black diminished and were succeeded by the blue and the blue was generally succeeded by the yellow, and some, but at first very few, were white".[4]

Owen believed that his success at New Lanark demonstrated how a wholesome environment and firm management could change the character of people. A workforce who had been criticised previously as drunken, dishonest and lazy became a model of hard work, orderliness and sobriety. At the same time the mill was a huge business success. He argued therefore that society had it in its power to ensure that people were generally of 'good character': "Any general character, from the best to the worst, from the most ignorant to the most enlightened, may be given to any community, even to the world at large, by the application of proper means; which means are to a great extent at the command and under the control of those who have influence in the affairs of men".[5]

He believed that education was essential so that children are trained "from their earliest infancy in good habits of every description".[6] Thus provision of education was part of the process of getting the environment right for the formation of good character. If society understands and acts upon its ability to ensure that living conditions and education are such that people are upright, honest and industrious then individuals will learn that "the happiness of self, clearly understood and uniformly practised...can only be attained by conduct that must promote the happiness of the community".[7]

New Lanark was in a sense a laboratory in which Owen developed and tested certain ideas. As his thinking evolved he came to advocate the establishment of 'Villages of Unity and Mutual Co-operation' as the best means of creating the right environment for the development of 'good character' within an economically sound and sustainable framework. His plan envisaged villages with a population of between 500 and 1,500 people, with housing built in the shape of a parallelogram, with public buildings in the centre. He later advocated collective dining facilities for all inhabitants and doing away with kitchen facilities in each house. He came to believe that the private ownership of property prevented improvement of the human condition and also that personal profit-making encouraged bad rather than good character. He aimed to do away with a social and economic system based on individual responsibility for self and replace it with one which recognised both the collective responsibility of society for how people are and the responsibility of individuals to their community. His village plan would create the ideal environment in which future generations could grow and develop.

At the same time as attacking competitive profit-seeking practices of 'buying cheap and selling dear', Owen also developed his ideas of a just price for the exchange of goods and services to be based on the labour-time required to make a particular product or perform a service. He proposed that 'labour notes' would replace the need for currency and ensure a fairer distribution of wealth.

Owen saw his community plan as being especially relevant initially to the poor and the oppressed and in his *Report to the County of Lanark*[8] he advocated starting to implement his plan amongst "those who are now a burden to the Country for want of employment". However he went on to argue that other sections in society will be so impressed by the "effects which will thus be produced on the character and circumstances of the oppressed class" that they "may place themselves under the new arrangements, when they have the evidence before them that these offer greater advantages than the old".

Promoting Owenism and co-operation

From 1818 Owen devoted much of his time, energy and wealth to promoting his ideas, going on lecture tours, forming fund-raising organisations, publishing tracts and periodicals, and initiating experiments to try out his ideas. From 1825 to 1827 he was in America setting up co-operative communities at New Harmony in Indiana and later in Texas. Other community experiments were attempted at Orbiston, near Glasgow (1825 - 1827) and at Queenwood, Hampshire (1839 - 1845). None survived for long despite Owen's personal energetic involvement in the first and last.

His ideas nevertheless found many enthusiastic supporters. The London Co-operative Society was set up in the 1820s to promote Owen's ideas and to raise funds to buy land on which to establish a community. Dr King in Brighton evolved the pragmatic approach whereby the starting point was a co-operative retail store, providing commodities needed by members and dealing only in cash. Profits would be used to set up individual members manufacturing items for sale. Further profits would be reinvested to employ more people and make more goods. Eventually "all the members would be self-employed through their society, and as they would have the whole product of their labour their capital would increase even faster. They would be able to purchase land and produce their own foodstuffs, build their own houses, provide their own schools, maintain sick and aged members and feed, clothe and educate members' children. The society would thus evolve into a community".[9]

In the 1830s Owen established a system of National Equitable Labour Exchanges to give practical force to his ideas of labour notes to establish true and fair prices for goods and services. The aim was to undermine commercial retailing and replace it by a system which enabled artisans to exchange articles for goods deposited by others, the value based on the labour needed for each article plus the cost of raw materials. In practice the exchanges clogged up with goods which could not be sold elsewhere and did not succeed.[10]

During 1832-34 Owen became involved in the establishment of the Grand Consolidated Trades Union of Great Britain and Ireland. His idea was to persuade workers to form national units of production which would intertrade using his fair labour note system. Working people had other ideas however and a series of strikes against local employers led to the arrest and trial of the Tolpuddle martyrs and the collapse of the union in 1834. The collapse took with it the Labour Exchanges and much of the pre-Rochdale co-operative movement which by then existed.

Owen, aged 64 but indefatigable, pressed on with promoting his ideas and ideals. He launched a new journal, the *New Moral World*, and founded the Universal Community Society of Rational Religionists (the Rational Society). From 1841 the Owenites tended to call themselves 'socialists', an annual congress was inaugurated and branches began to spread throughout the country. Meetings, lectures and discussions were held by the local branches on a widening range of ideas, thinking and issues. 'Social missionaries' toured the country. The House of Lords debated the 'Owenite menace'. The seeds for social change were being extensively sown. And out of No 24 branch of the Rational Society grew the Rochdale Society of Equitable Pioneers. "They took their affairs into their own hands, and what is more to the purpose, they kept them in their own hands."[11]

Owen was seeking to do away with poverty and destitution, to ensure that all people could lead healthy and happy lives, in harmony with each other and with their surroundings. He understood that external factors determine the lot of the majority of individuals and that collectively man can, and must, exert beneficent control and influence over the environments in which people live and work. He recognised that a focus on private profit cannot lead to collective benefit. He sought an educated and enlightened population, producing enough for their wants but not wasting time and energy on over-production nor on unnecessary individual wealth creation.

These ideas of collective action for mutual benefit are part of the heritage on which the modern community enterprise movement is based. It is idealistic in that it seeks a different way of running human affairs at all levels but it is practical and pragmatic in the way of Dr King and of the Rochdale Pioneers, in that it understands the need to start with a viable practical operation and to build from there.

There is much that can be usefully learned by understanding something of the history. To the present day community enterpriser it is interesting to note how the Rochdale Pioneers started in a very small way, essentially as a 'voluntary enterprise' and grew slowly over a considerable period of time. The idea of joint ventures between societies and members of one society becoming part of other societies with other purposes but within a common philosophical framework has considerable relevance to present issues under discussion within the community enterprise movement. Similarly it is interesting to note how the key objectives of an organisation can be subverted if they are not in some way entrenched, an issue discussed in chapter 12. It is also relevant to note that Bonner[12] records as some of the other reasons for the failure of the early co-operative societies the failure to keep good accounts and failure of lay management committees to understand their business properly and thus being unable to exert effective control over the society's staff. Plus ça change: see chapter 7.

Idealism was the driving force behind the early co-operative movement. Although the aim of establishing an Owenite community was dropped, the commitment to social objectives such as education, fair trading and sharing profits with members remained firm over the generations. In working class areas the co-op is remembered as much more than a shop, it was part of the fabric of society and the 'divi number' remains fixed in millions of British memories. Despite the great changes to the co-operative movement and to society over the years, that idealism remains part of present day co-operative organisation. The Co-operative Bank has been the first of the banks to publicise its ethical and environmental policies: "We can show that behaviour that is unacceptable to society should not be acceptable in business".[13]

The importance of idealism in community enterprise and the balance which must be achieved between commercial reality and social idealism is a theme which has consumed considerable energy in debate over the past two decades and which will be further examined later.

Chapter 3

A question of values: definitions and all that

"If there be one closet doctrine more contrary to truth than another, it is the notion that individual interest, as that term is now understood, is a more advantageous principle on which to found the social system, for the benefit of all, than the principle of union and mutual co-operation."

The generic term community enterprise is comfortably used to include different types of community organisation including Development Trusts, Community Businesses and Community Co-operatives.

It is also generally agreed that credit unions and community-based housing associations and co-operatives are forms of community enterprise in that they share a common value base with the other organisations. They may be distinguished however in two ways. First, their respective functions are very precise and clear, and second, they come under a form of regulatory system: in the case of the credit unions via their own legislation and the Registry of Friendly Societies, and in the case of the housing organisations via the Housing Corporation (Scottish Homes).

The functions of the other community enterprises range from property development and managed workspace to environmental improvements, from running training programmes to running island shops, from building companies to security services, from food co-operatives to thrift shops, from painting and decorating to tourism services, from childcare to community cafes. **Figure ii** is taken from a leaflet produced by Community Business Scotland to depict the wide range of activities in which Scottish community enterprises are engaged. The list is endless and it is this very catholicity of function which gives rise to spirited debate and disagreement within the community enterprise movement about what community enterprises should and should not do, and therefore what their purpose is.

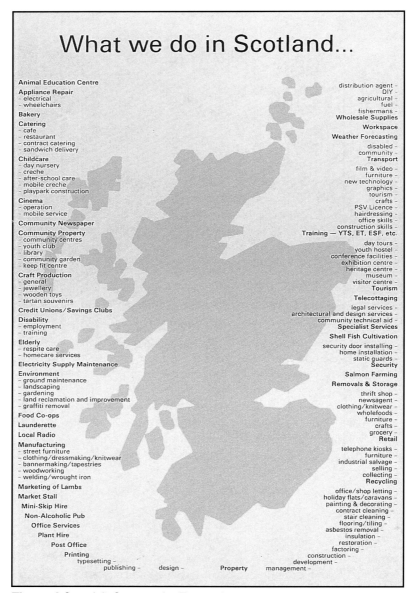

What we do in Scotland...

Animal Education Centre	distribution agent –
Appliance Repair	DIY –
– electrical	agricultural –
– wheelchairs	fuel –
Bakery	fishermans –
Catering	Wholesale Supplies
– cafe	Workspace
– restaurant	Weather Forecasting
– contract catering	disabled –
– sandwich delivery	community –
Childcare	Transport
– day nursery	film & video –
– creche	furniture –
– after-school care	new technology –
– mobile creche	graphics –
– playpark construction	tourism –
Cinema	crafts –
– operation	PSV Licence –
– mobile service	hairdressing –
Community Newspaper	office skills –
Community Property	construction skills –
– community centres	Training — YTS, ET, ESF, etc.
– youth club	day tours –
– library	youth hostel –
– community garden	conference facilities –
– keep fit centre	exhibition centre –
Craft Production	heritage centre –
– general	museum –
– jewellery	visitor centre –
– wooden toys	Tourism
– tartan souvenirs	Telecottaging
Credit Unions/Savings Clubs	legal services –
Disability	architectural and design services –
– employment	community technical aid –
– training	Specialist Services
Elderly	Shell Fish Cultivation
– respite care	security door installing –
– homecare services	home installation –
Electricity Supply Maintenance	static guards –
Environment	Security
– ground maintenance	Salmon Farming
– landscaping	Removals & Storage
– gardening	thrift shop –
– land reclamation and improvement	newsagent –
– graffiti removal	clothing/knitwear –
Food Co-ops	wholefoods –
Launderette	furniture –
Local Radio	crafts –
Manufacturing	grocery –
– street furniture	Retail
– clothing/dressmaking/knitwear	telephone kiosks –
– bannermaking/tapestries	furniture –
– woodworking	industrial salvage –
– welding/wrought iron	selling –
Marketing of Lambs	collecting –
Market Stall	Recycling
Mini-Skip Hire	office/shop letting –
Non-Alcoholic Pub	holiday flats/caravans –
Office Services	painting & decorating –
Plant Hire	contract cleaning –
Post Office	stair cleaning –
Printing	flooring/tiling –
typesetting –	asbestos removal –
publishing – design –	insulation –
Property	restoration –
management –	factoring –
	construction –
	development –

Figure i Scottish Community Enterprises

However, if we look first at the key characteristics which appear to underpin all types of community enterprise organisation, we find that there is a good measure of common ground. In the appendices can be found three recent definitions of community enterprise produced by:

1. Community Business Scotland (December 1991)

2. Business in the Community: Investing in Community Enterprise Initiative (February 1992)

3. Development Trusts Association (Spring 1992)

It is the common ground between these three definitions which is striking. The key characteristics may be summarised as follows:

● They are **community owned** in that the assets belong to the designated community and may not be sold off for individual financial gain.

● They are **community-led** in that people who are local stake-holders in the area of benefit, and not the local authority or any other dominant interest, play a leading role in the initiative. In this sense they are independent.

● They are **community controlled** in that their constitutions ensure an effective mechanism whereby the local community is represented on the Board of Directors and whereby the enterprise and its Board are *accountable* to its community.

● They do **not distribute any surplus** to members or to directors: surplus is strictly for re-investment or for community benefit.

● They are concerned to do something about the **economic, social and environmental** problems facing their area.

● They aim to become **financially self-sustaining** from their various activities.

There are three main ways in which Community Enterprises can therefore be distinguished from private enterprise:

1. Community Enterprise has social objectives to benefit the community: indeed any business activity is undertaken as the chosen **means of achieving community benefit**.

2. Profit, which is essential to the sustainability of the enterprise, together with increasing wealth and asset value belong to the community and not to individuals: **common-ownership**.

3. There is an **effective system of accountability** to the community, usually incorporating some form of democratic structure.

The nature of community is discussed in some detail later (chapter 5). However it is appropriate to note here that the usual interpretation of community in relation to community enterprise is a geographical one where there is a sense of identity with a particular area. Although this cannot be exactly prescribed in terms of population or square miles, a sense of 'localness' is important. A second interpretation of community concerns a group of people with a common need or interest which acts as their 'common bond' rather than residence or employment in an area. Even so, in most cases where a community of interest or need is agreed it will be appropriate also to apply a test of 'localness' so that the 'community' consists of people with a common interest or need within an agreed district. Such districts may be larger than those of the geographically-based community enterprises and indeed may overlay those areas without causing confusion or conflict because of the specialist nature of the 'common bond'.

It is never entirely clear whether worker co-operatives can be considered to be community enterprises or not. Essentially the choice is that of any particular worker co-operative which believes it can subscribe to the basic characteristics and values of community enterprise. For many common-ownership worker co-operatives their constitution already precludes the realisation of assets for distribution amongst working members: they are held in common and in trust for succeeding generations of workers. For many worker co-operatives engagement with and accountability to the local community is also very much part of their philosophy and working practice. The key issue is the use of the profits generated: do they belong exclusively to the worker members who can decide to share them out amongst themselves only or is there a commitment not only to re-invest but also to allocate some profit to community benefit?

The Scott Bader Commonwealth which has pioneered much innovation in worker ownership in Britain since the early 1960s has a carefully worded constitution which ensures that at least 60% of profit is placed into company reserves (for re-investment and to secure the business for future generations of workers) with the balance being the maximum distributable amount to be equally divided between bonus payments to the workforce and investment in community benefit.[1] In their case community investment is via the Scott Bader Commonwealth Development Foundation which is managed by representatives of the workforce and which has a long-standing record of supporting community projects and in particular assisting the establishment of new worker co-operative initiatives.

At the other extreme will be those worker-owned businesses which, while adopting an internal democratic structure, exist first and foremost to maximise the income and return for their working members. Such 'democratic associations of capitalists' are more likely to align themselves with the conventional small business sector than with the ideals of the community enterprise sector.

Enterprise and business

The term community business (originally, Community Business Ventures) was born on the day in 1980 when Jim Prior, then Secretary of State for Employment in Margaret Thatcher's first government, decided to adopt the name 'Community Enterprise Programme' (CEP) for the latest phase of the temporary work schemes. These had started life under the previous Labour administration of the late 1970s as the Job Creation Programme (JCP) (probably the most apt name of all), became the Special Temporary Employment Programme (STEP), then the CEP before ending up as the late (and quite lamented) Community Programme which was replaced by Employment Training (ET) in 1988.

Until Jim Prior 'hi-jacked' the term, 'Community Enterprise' had been used as the generic title for all those growing development attempts rooted in the local community to contribute to regeneration by creating jobs and providing services. The forerunner to Community Business Scotland had, for example, been the Scottish Community Enterprise Forum. It was only since the relatively recent demise of the CEP and its successor the Community Programme that the term Community Enterprise has been 'rehabilitated'.

'Enterprise' is a good word: it is implicitly to do with initiative, with building a capacity to take action, about learning new skills, about working out how to tackle a problem, about taking risks ("disposition to engage in undertakings of difficulty, risk or danger": *Shorter Oxford English Dictionary SOED*). 'Community Business' which replaced the term Community Enterprise has a much narrower connotation which tends to concentrate on the profit and loss and on the balance sheet outcomes. Enterprise can be - and should be - applied to all areas of life while business is really only to do with the pursuit of profit ("commercial transactions or engagements": *SOED*).

The use of the word 'business' in Community Business has tended to imply the establishment only of trading organisations which will be commercially profitable entirely through their trading activities. This 'business' rather than an 'enterprise' focus has diverted attention from the understanding that Community Business is but one of a number of possible outcomes from a local development process. That process is community development in its proper sense, where all needs and aspects of a community must be considered, recognising the inter-connectedness of problems and possibilities. That is particularly important in areas of deprivation where the relationships between unemployment, poverty, education, health and housing are entirely intertwined.

Community development: community building

In North America the term community development is taken to mean just that: the development of the community: housing, infrastructure, business, social and welfare services, training and education. That same holistic approach is to be found in the Canadian Community Futures Programmes where representative community committees are formed to plan the future based on an analysis of the needs and aspirations of all sectors of the community. In the UK, community development has tended to restrict itself (or to be restricted) to matters to do with the environment, with housing, with welfare services, with campaigns and advocacy but seldom to do with the local economy and employment and training development. British community development has also been characterised by taking an issue-based approach rather than an integrated, holistic approach and in this it follows the bureaucratic compartmentalisation of government, both local and central. Think for a moment of the various departments of a local authority that might claim to have a community development strategy and workers to go with it, and then add on those from the voluntary sector with a similar remit.

Coin Street Community Builders of Waterloo on London's South Bank are not a building company in the construction industry sense. They have set out to rebuild their community, acting as a local development organisation concerned with community development in the broad sense.

It is that understanding of community development that has influenced much community enterprise thinking in Britain. The Community Enterprise Model (**figure iii**) which was first developed by the Local Enterprise Advisory Project (LEAP) in the late 1970s illustrates the concept of the Community Enterprise acting as a 'Local Development Agency', in part running businesses and projects directly and in part facilitating the formation and growth of other elements of the community economy.

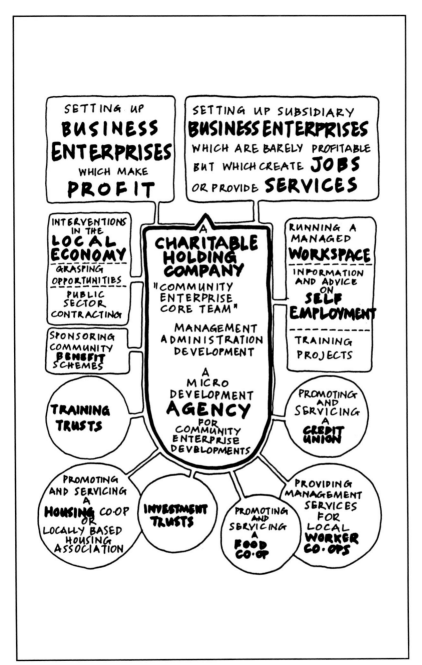

Figure iii Community Enterprise Model

Community development which begins by addressing the wide range of problem issues facing any community will inevitably find itself addressing the issue of unemployment and the need to regenerate the local economy. The ability of members of a community to earn an adequate living is the basis on which community viability is founded; and a community where a significant proportion of the residents is out of work and dependent on state benefits can quickly show the symptoms of decline which are all too familiar in our cities and in the remoter regions of the countryside. While there are those, mostly connected to the present government, who will deny any link between poverty and unemployment on the one hand and social disturbance and community malaise on the other, those who live and work in areas of 'disadvantage' are quite clear in their minds about the causal connection.

Community development which starts from the basis of the needs and aspirations of the local community will, by definition, be people-centred. That is, the value of the development will ultimately be measured by the beneficial (or otherwise) impact on the people of the area. Sensitivity to people must also embrace sensitivity to the planet: otherwise we shall continue to degrade our living environment and risk passing on to future (and not so distant) generations an unsustainable world.

Social, economic or integrated?

In Scotland, where community enterprise has had its most overt support from local and central government since the middle 1970s, the concept emerged out of social strategy thinking. The HIDB community co-operative scheme (1977) was located in the Social Development Section of the Highlands and Islands Development Board.[2] In Strathclyde, community enterprise was adopted for main-line council funding (1983) as part of its social strategy, the Council reflecting the conventional divergence of social and economic with a separate strategy and sub-committee for each.

The urban programme from which significant funding for community enterprise has been provided, especially north of the border, was essentially a social development initiative, created by the Wilson government initially in response to Enoch Powell's 'rivers of blood' speech and the concern over urban poverty and the perceived danger of social disruption. More recently its focus has shifted to the 'economic' based on the understanding that social problems may also be addressed through initiatives which include an economic development component. The very recent Government initiative of City Challenge has taken farther the trend towards a holistic approach to development, setting out to solve a range of local problems with an integrated approach based on the concept of partnership. That integrated approach has been the hallmark of community enterprise, despite the public sector needing to 'pigeonhole' it; first as 'social', more recently as 'economic'. In fact it is, and must be, both.

A business development scheme which ignores the skill levels of local people and the problems of getting the long-term unemployed back into work will have little direct success with the people most in need. A scheme to revitalise the housing and landscape the environment will be of small consolation to people if they must grind along in poverty and debt with their children poorly educated and unlikely to find work. These community realities are the context in which community enterprises work: indeed the community enterprise movement has developed more as a means of creating development in poor disadvantaged communities, rather than as a method of creating jobs and businesses alone.

Where the community enterprise is seen as a structure which allows a community development process to take place, there are a range of outcomes which might be anticipated:

- community businesses
- property development
- land and environmental developments
- training programmes
- information and advice services
- job creation schemes
- local community services
- assisting other discrete forms of community enterprise to develop within the local community economy: housing co-operatives, worker co-operatives, credit unions.

The community enterprise model illustrated in **figure iii** shows a core team which has both a development and a management capacity. As an organisation it might directly manage a range of businesses or projects, illustrated within the boxes in the upper half of the diagram. Few, if any, community enterprises will be so multi-functional as to actually carry out all of the activities shown and in most real life situations a community enterprise will concentrate on a few activities, or sometimes only one.

As local development agent the community enterprise may become involved in facilitating the creation of other activities in the community economy which are illustrated within the circles in the diagram. These, as they become established, may or may not retain an ongoing structural or support relationship with the 'core community enterprise'.

The core community enterprise might be especially created for the purpose, or it might evolve from an existing community-based organisation: a community business, a community-based housing association, a housing co-operative, a community organisation which decides to adopt an integrated approach to development combining the economic and the social.

Models have the advantage of conceptually simplifying ideas, but they also make things appear neat and tidy. The real world, and people in particular, is not neat and tidy and ready to drop into the appropriate box

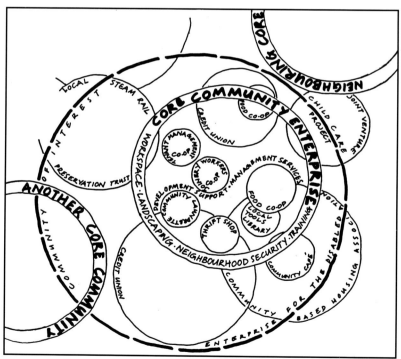

Figure iv Community Enterprise in Action

or circle. To be useful the model has to allow flexible interpretation and implementation. In a real situation it may be that several community enterprises will emerge to do different things in the local community economy. Some will be linked and mutually supportive; others will be fiercely independent. Their areas of benefit may vary. **Figure iv** attempts to illustrate the real life community economy with what can appear to be a confusing muddle of enterprises and projects.

Within the real life confusion it is helpful to identify a 'core community enterprise' which will undertake the development function: to facilitate the development of other parts of the community economy and to encourage the development of people ('capacity building'). A further important role for the core community enterprise is to develop links between different parts of the community economy, to encourage mutual support, sharing of resources and inter-working. It is important to recognise these development tasks of the core community enterprise and to understand that seldom can they be financed from the business activities of the enterprise. That means they require to be paid for externally.

The community business continuum

In chapter 4 we shall explore in some detail the market opportunities which it seems community enterprises are especially suited to. However it is appropriate to note here that community businesses are but one community enterprise outcome from the community development process. Within the business activities which might be gathered under the general heading of Community Business it is more useful to understand that there is a continuum (**figure v**) of trading which ranges from **Voluntary Enterprises** to **Social Enterprises** to **Community Businesses**, where:

A **Voluntary Enterprise** is a project to provide a local service which is run in a business-like fashion but which uses for the most part volunteer labour. Examples of Voluntary Enterprises would include Thrift Shops, Food Co-operatives, Community Credit Unions, much child-care provision, a Senior Citizens Lunch Club.

A **Social Enterprise** is a business providing a social or commercial service which requires some ongoing special contract arrangement or subsidy, usually from the public sector, or from within the Community Enterprise Group, or in the form of some unpaid labour input. Examples of a Social Enterprise would include: a pensioners' hair-cutting service where Social Work pays a per capita contribution;

workspaces and other property projects with a peppercorn rent arrangement; childcare schemes where premises and other facilities are provided free of charge or where there is a special arrangement with one company or institution guaranteeing a percentage of the places; a community-run swimming pool where the local council contributes towards the revenue costs; neighbourhood caretaking and security contracts which are specially negotiated; island shops which depend on some voluntary labour to help out.

A **Community Business** is a business which should become viable and sustainable without any ongoing external assistance, beyond that which is generally available as part of small business support schemes.

Figure v The Community Business Continuum

Movement along the continuum will and should happen, but it is important not to set up as a Community Business something that can never be more than a Voluntary Enterprise. For example, most thrift shops and community cafes are likely to be Voluntary Enterprises but some may become a Social Enterprise and, in exceptional circumstances, a Community Business. Some projects like these and others like community launderettes may operate in different ways at different times: sometimes paying staff, sometimes dependent on volunteers, sometimes breaking even, sometimes not. It is important to be realistic about the potential of a project when planning it and target aspirations accordingly. Trying to set up as a Community Business something which can only realistically be a Voluntary Enterprise will only serve to give those involved, and outside sponsors, a sense and perception of failure as they see the Community Business 'decline' into a Voluntary Enterprise, or close down entirely.

Equally it is important to recognise the value of running an efficient service as a Social Enterprise and not denigrate it simply because it cannot become a commercially viable Community Business. (After all we happily subsidise rural bus services and upland sheep farmers, and most arms manufacturers depend on government contracts from which they have managed to make reasonable profits over the years.)

38

The continuum must be dynamic and permit shifts along it by projects and people in both directions at different times. In development terms the capacity to learn in one category and move on to another is a vital part of the process. In economic terms all types of 'business' along the continuum are trading organisations and make an important and valuable contribution to the community economy.

A sustainable balance

The balance between community benefit and commercial trading is at the heart of community enterprise. A sustainable balance is simply one that allows a community enterprise to earn through all its activities sufficient revenue to meet its expenditure, allow for depreciation and build up reserves (**figure vi**). Whether that revenue comes in the form of sales in the market place, payment because society contracts with the enterprise to do something, or grants because that is the way government, local authority or charitable trusts prefer to pay, or internal cross-subsidisation from profitable to non-profitable within the Community Enterprise Group, should not be relevant, provided that, taken as a whole, each Community Enterprise Group can pay its way. Revenue, whatever form it takes, is (or should be) payment for making or doing something. The clearer the contract on which each deal is based, the less scope for some payments being seen as support for business inefficiency.

This is especially relevant when the community enterprise is seen as a Local Development Organisation. The original model envisaged that sufficient successful business could be developed to generate adequate surplus to finance the core costs of **both** management and development staff (**figure iii**). It has only been in exceptional circumstances that this has proved to be possible. Coin Street Community Builders, with revenue earned from car-parking on land it owns, has been able to sustain its core development costs entirely independently. The North Kensington Amenity Trust now finds itself in the enviable position of earning sufficient revenue from its commercial lettings to be able to fund both its core management and its development costs and make £65,000 of grants annually to local community organisations. But it was not always so and the early developmental years in their history depended on grant-aid from a range of sources.

The Allander Group has been consistently profitable for four years and is therefore able to apply its reserves to development. Govan

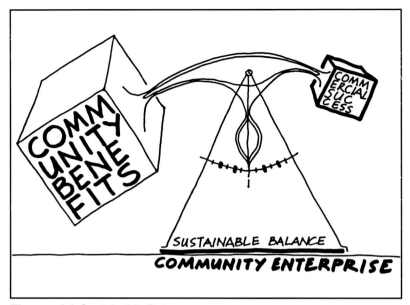

Figure vi A Sustainable Balance

Workspace has successfully outlived its period of revenue urban aid grant support and is now able to survive commercially, although the current recession and down-turn in small business activity means that there is currently less resource free for development than the company would have expected. By contrast the Eldonian Group in Vauxhall, despite the great success of its individual projects, still finds itself having to seek support from both public and private sectors to finance its development team.

The Eldonian experience is the rule rather than the exception. Not surprisingly many community enterprises have found it impossible to earn enough from their business activities to sustain a local development role. It has been difficult enough in most cases ensuring that business and project activities, taken together, can properly fund the effective management they need. Again that is not surprising, with the benefit of hindsight.

For the most part community enterprises are trying to create viable businesses in some of the most disadvantaged communities in the country and aiming to employ in those businesses local long-term unemployed people. They tend to become involved in activities which are labour intensive and with low profit margins. These are the

40

unpropitious circumstances in which community enterprises operate, and the very ones which private business for the most part avoids. That some community enterprises have succeeded and survived is more than creditable. That few have made the sort of profits that can fund community benefit and community development is entirely unsurprising.

Those that have failed and been closed down have been judged on a profit and loss basis rather than a 'value added' or 'savings to the public purse' basis, a theme which is explored further in the chapter on Auditing the Community Benefit (chapter 12).

In Scotland the community enterprise movement's own claims about what to expect multi-functional community enterprises to be able to sustain can be seen to have been over-optimistic and even, with hindsight, naive; even if it was to some degree fostered by the sort of 'soft' earnings that community enterprises were able to earn through involvement with the Manpower Service Commission's job creation schemes. By the early claims many community enterprises must be judged to have failed. What we can now understand is that the claims and expectations were unreasonable and the subsequent judgement of performance misguided. If community enterprises are to act as local development agencies then they must be contracted to provide that service. Similarly if they do provide community benefit which is valuable to the local community and to wider society then that benefit must be acknowledged, measured and paid for by society.

The national and international trend has been towards performance measurement based only on factors to which a cost can be given. This market economy approach is now pervading the whole of our public services and its application to community enterprise has meant that effectively only two factors are judged important and worthwhile: How many jobs have been created? and, Is the business commercially viable?

Community development or business development?

In Scotland a consequence has been to eschew the community development model of community enterprise and to concentrate on community business development and, in terms of the continuum described earlier, especially on the commercially viable end. Thus support for businesses which fall into the Voluntary Enterprise or Social Enterprise categories are specifically ruled out by some of

Scotland's community enterprise development units. This response is understandable: it is difficult to stand against the tide of opinion and legislation which puts profit before people and against the conventional wisdom of economic thinking which does not recognise much of the community economy. The problem is exacerbated by community enterprises being judged on their own exaggerated claims of a decade ago.

The argument in favour of community enterprise concentrating exclusively and single-mindedly on profitable business creation is that the community enterprise sector will only gain credibility with the public and private sectors by playing and winning according to their rules. Once that has been achieved and enterprises under community ownership are successfully competing in the market place, then the community enterprise sector can move on to capture 'the commanding heights' and start to change the rules in its favour. Others, more cynical, interpret the drive to commercially viable business alone as a pragmatic response to living within the rules as they have been recast during the years of the 'enterprise culture' and understand that conquering the commanding heights is more to do with political change than with community business start-up.

The key question was expressed vividly in a turmoil of exasperation by a senior worker in one of Scotland's development units: "Are we about creating community enterprises or about setting up businesses in poor communities?"

Chapter 4 explores the type of work for which the community enterprise model seems to have been most appropriate and concludes that community enterprise is especially relevant to the community economy. That is not to say that the values on which community enterprise is based: common-ownership, people before profit, are not relevant to other 'layers' in the economy. There are however other political, legislative and structural ways of bringing the other layers more under the influence of those values: community enterprise is a structure for the community economy.

The long-term view is that community enterprise, together with other elements of the community economy such as community-based housing associations and co-operatives and credit unions, is part of a community development process which is predicated on a different value base from current government thinking and from prevailing business ethos. It is therefore essential that community enterprise holds to its holistic approach to development and to its continuum approach to business development. Although this is different from conventional wisdom it does not necessarily have to be in conflict with it. Indeed it will be argued later that community enterprise as a development model not only complements the public and private sectors, but could be an essential part of the development and regeneration jigsaw which it is in all our interests to complete.

Chapter 4

Community enterprise markets: "touching the life of the neighbourhood"

"The waste of capital and labour, by unnecessary establishments, and by the production of useless or injurious articles, created to tempt society to purchase them, are small evils compared to the extent of the injurious feelings, violent passions, vices and miseries unavoidably attendant on a system of individual competition, and more especially when that competition is carried to the extent it has now attained in the financial world."

After nearly two decades of community enterprise growth and development in Britain it is possible to examine the areas of trading and other activity in which community enterprises have become established in order to see if there are any perceptible trends. It is also relevant to consider what other appropriate market opportunities might be either currently available or likely to emerge in the future.

An examination of Community Enterprise experience suggests that they are good at the following:

1. Creating and managing workspace, usually aimed especially at new start enterprises and providing the advice, training and support infrastructure which is necessary to help people set up and sustain their own small businesses

Often the workspace is created in old, redundant buildings which are suitably converted. Workshops are for the most part small so that businesses only need to rent the amount of space which they actually need, and for most new starts that is usually quite modest, perhaps the size of a single garage, sometimes even smaller. Leases are on an easy-in easy-out basis (usually monthly) to minimise the risk for tenants and in addition to the business support services the workspace will offer a range of practical services such as toilets, secure parking, buildings maintenance and insurance, security, caretaking, cleaning of common areas, reception, fax, telex and copying: all designed to give tenant businesses the most advantageous working environment at reasonable, but commercial, rents and at minimum bother.

Probably the best known community enterprise workspace is Govan Workspace in Glasgow with its 140,000 square feet of workshops in the three buildings which it now owns. Other innovative workspace developments have included the conversion of former housing stock and lock-up garages into small blocks of workspace in what was formerly a wholly residential area and the development of derelict land under a motorway flyover.

2. Acting as the developer for a range of properties or an area to develop a mix of housing, commercial/industrial, community and environmental uses

This has been the main activity for a number of the larger American Community Development Corporations, often beginning with the provision of social housing, reflecting the different tradition across the Atlantic as regards the provision of social housing. CDCs such as the Watts Community Labor Action Committee in Los Angeles became involved in other schemes of property and environmental development, including the provision of community facilities, and ensuring that job and training opportunities for local people are included both in the development phases themselves and in the final outcome of the developments.

The most publicised and probably the most successful example of this approach in Britain so far has been the North Kensington Amenity Trust and its development of the 23 acres of wasteland under the raised section of the M40 in west London. Another example, also described earlier, is the Loftus Development Trust (LDT) in rural East Cleveland.

3. Running training programmes targeted at the local population

The advantage which community enterprises have demonstrated as training providers is the ability to successfully target those least likely to present themselves for training. This requires a flexible approach which can tailor-make programmes to fit the needs of the local population and most usually this has to begin with what has recently become known as 'capacity building': helping people gain confidence, develop a sense of worth, recognise that they have and can acquire skills, build a motivation to do rather than be done to. It is not possible to over-emphasise the importance of this first stage of training for the long-term unemployed, including, as it should, 'remedial' help with basic skills such as literacy and numeracy which are all too often found to be lacking.

Being locally rooted the community enterprise can be well placed to deliver this preliminary type of training - almost preparation for training - and then to build onto it real work experience and appropriate vocational training to help people get into the labour market with the sort of skills that are in demand. The Finsbury Park Community Trust has made this latter stage one of its main areas of activity working very closely with private sector companies who use the Trust as their agents to recruit and train new personnel from amongst the unemployed in north London.

British training policy has tended to move its recent focus onto the acquisition of vocational skills to a recognised paper standard. While this makes sense in terms of common and accepted standards it has resulted in a withdrawal of resources from the vital first stage: capacity building, largely it would seem because it is harder to measure outputs and to fit it into a market system of payment. The gap has been partly filled by the European Social Fund, but that source is always problematic for community-based organisations which lack the cash-flow resource to tide them over against the always delayed final payment, even if they have been successful in obtaining matching public sector funding, completing the abstruse application forms with the appropriate buzz words and financial calculations, and have an adequate administration system to keep the intricate records needed for a possible visit from the EC auditors!

4. Running job creation schemes especially geared to getting the long-term unemployed back into work and acquiring some skills so that they can rejoin the mainstream labour market

The now defunct Community Programme (CP) (and its predecessors) was the main vehicle used by community enterprises to get local long-term unemployed people back to work and doing useful work of community benefit at the same time. It was an area of operation at which community enterprises were very effective and many managed to ensure that a reasonable element of training was included in the projects for which they were responsible.

What the job creation programmes such as CP recognised, perhaps by chance, was that it is not a straightforward process to get the long-term unemployed back to work. To survive being long-term unemployed, people have to adjust to the condition of not working. When that has been the norm for a lengthy period, it is just as much a 'shock to the system' to start work again as it is to someone in work to be told they are no longer wanted. When unemployment is the local cultural norm, as too often it is in the run-down estates and inner-city areas, and where it has become a generational condition 'like father like son', then the cycle is even harder to break.

Community Programme schemes helped to break that cycle and schemes run by community enterprises were often particularly successful in that good workers could be fed on through the community enterprise system to more commercial areas of activity once the basic patterns of regular work had been re-established and, not unusually, physical fitness had been regained. This 'throughput' was both to commercial business within the community enterprise group and to other employers.

Regrettably the trend towards the end of the CP scheme had been to move away from small providers in favour of a limited number of big providers (managing agents as they were known). The same trend has happened with Employment Training (which replaced the CP). While it may be administratively neater and cheaper to run a programme such as CP through a small number of agents, for best results on the ground it is preferable to work through a larger number of smaller local organisations. This is of course the principle of subsidiarity, a point to which we shall return later.

There was another, political, problem faced by a number of community enterprises at the time of transition from CP to ET, and also when Employment Action (EA) was introduced.[1] Some local authorities decided not to co-operate with ET and EA and that policy was effectively forced upon community enterprises within their areas which were dependent on the council for financial support, premises or contracts. While many in the community enterprise movement disliked ET and were especially hesitant about the 'Workfare' connotations of EA,[2] the better pragmatic reality would have been to explore some way of adjusting to ET without too much compromise rather than abrupt withdrawal on imposed political grounds.

5. Offering local services, often on contract to the public sector, which can be done by relatively unskilled and formerly unemployed local people and where it is both appropriate and beneficial for local people to do the work

There could be a moral imperative about the desirability of local people doing local work. On the one hand is the sense of outrage and frustration felt by unemployed people sitting in their houses and watching other people come in day by day to do work they know they could do: straightforward landscaping, estate caretaking, simple painting and decorating, cleaning out empty houses, neighbourhood security, graffiti removal...On the other is the recognised value of work being done by local people: a sense of ownership and pride, less vandalism, doing rather than waiting.

Community enterprises have made a speciality of providing these sorts of services and a number of local authorities have seen the relevance of engaging community enterprises to provide them. Glasgow District Council in particular led the way with contracts in neighbourhood security, landscaping and housing estate caretaking. Unfortunately the Government's Compulsory Competitive Tendering (CCT) legislation has made it progressively more difficult for local authorities to favour community enterprises: to do so would be to take non-commercial matters into consideration when awarding a contract.[3] In terms of the legislation employing local people, getting the unemployed back to work, encouraging feelings of pride, responsibility and ownership, reducing vandalism etc are all non-commercial considerations.

Over the years community enterprises have had good results in employing local people in doing local work. Unfortunately there has been no systematic research[4] into the impact on the persons employed, but anecdotal and impressionistic evidence suggests that people have been getting back to work with the local community enterprise and then moving on, perhaps a year or 18 months later, into jobs in the open labour market. It is always easier to get a job if they are already in work than if they are long-term unemployed, especially if their address is associated with an area of long-term unemployment and therefore unemployability.

Successful 'throughput' of this sort is by nature potentially damaging for the community enterprise working on a commercial contract in that it is constantly recruiting the less able from the ranks of the unemployed and helping get them back into the labour market. Productivity and efficiency cannot be good if a proportion of the labour force is unfit, quite unskilled and if some leniency has to be exercised while workers get re-accustomed to the discipline of a working day.

Again there has been no systematic research, but the impression is that one of the important factors which contributed to the commercial failure of some community enterprises in Scotland, notably in the areas of landscaping and general contracting, was their successful recruitment policy favouring the local long-term unemployed who subsequently obtained jobs with other contractors. In other words it is very hard to make a profit in areas of business where margins are anyway modest at the best of times and employ the sort of people other contractors avoid. Before CCT local authorities could compensate for this, after CCT such assistance is no longer possible. And yet the value not only of the employment throughput, but also of local people doing local work should be self evident.

Getting the long-term unemployed back to work is really a three stage process:

1. capacity building

2. acquiring the work pattern

3. vocational training

Community Enterprises have demonstrated their ability to do all three, but in particular one and two. However, it is necessary to recognise that successfully achieving stage two within the constraints of a commercial contract is virtually (though not always) impossible.[5] It is certainly unrealistic to plan in that way. Schemes such as the Community Programme or some form of 'soft' contract are appropriate. It is also important to recognise that stage three, vocational training, best follows on from stages one and two: individuals with a renewed sense of purpose and a renewed taste for work and an idea of what they would like to do will make infinitely better trainees when they understand the relevance of the training they are to undertake.

6. Running local commercial services which the private sector cannot make pay

The most common example is probably the island or village shop, given up by the former operator as not making sufficient profit, but revived by the community because it is a service essential to individual householders and to the general well-being - indeed survival - of the community.

Other examples include craft co-operatives, retailing small holding and fishermen's supplies, small holiday home networks and guest house accommodation, electricity generation, local Post Office, community cafes, telecottaging, local transport, petrol station...

Sometimes the community enterprise will manage to make profitable the business which the private sector has given up on. More often it will accept lower profitability or indeed will achieve viability by means of some voluntary labour or other support or by running the business as part of a network of other businesses.

While many of these types of business are more usually associated with rural community enterprises, there is potentially just as important a role for them in urban areas, particularly if the notion of the community business continuum (**figure v**) is acknowledged and accepted.

7. Providing care services where quality of care should be as or more important than the profit margin

The most common area of care work in which community enterprises have so far become involved is childcare. Ironically it is virtually impossible to run a childcare business on a strictly commercial basis and benefit those most in need from areas of poverty and high unemployment: the poor cannot afford the true cost of effective childcare. It is therefore necessary to find ways in which costs can be subsidised in order to offer reduced cost places or to enter into partnership arrangements with the private sector either to sponsor places or to guarantee the purchase of some places so that an equivalent number can be offered to local people at an affordable price. A good example of this type of arrangement is the deal struck with Littlewoods plc by the Eldonian Development Trust in Liverpool in a joint venture to set up a nursery to meet the needs both of the community and of the company which is located nearby.

The Eldonians have also shown the way in the field of residential care of the elderly with Eldonian House, a home for 32 old people next door to the Eldonian Village on the site of the old Tate and Lyle refinery. The home, a joint venture with a specialist housing association, caters mostly for local old people from the Vauxhall area. Nearly all the staff of the home are local which means that the old folk are cared for by people they have known all their lives. Also, being local and community-based, permits relatives to call in regularly and to continue helping to care for their elderly relative.

Government policy with regard to community care is going to see a growth in caring services being put out to contract to be provided by organisations and agencies other than the local authorities. The principle behind this move is that the role of the state should be to set standards and ensure that services are provided, but not necessarily to provide them itself. There is surely another moral imperative here, namely that such services preferably be provided by organisations (such as community enterprises) more concerned about quality than about profit margin. Also the principle of subsidiarity argues in favour of service provision at the local, community level.

Community enterprise could be an important vehicle for the provision of local caring services: to ensure this there are two essential and related requirements. First, that the public sector agencies responsible for placing contracts must decide that community provision using the community enterprise structure will be a good way of doing things and specify contracts accordingly, with reference in particular to size of contracts. Second, they must ensure that specialist training and guidance is made available so that existing or, more likely, newly created community enterprises can acquire the expertise they will require both with regard to tendering and to fulfilling contracts effectively. It will not be enough to simply put contracts out into the open market place where price will inevitably be the over-riding consideration. It will be essential to modify the market to ensure that quality is the main consideration and that community-based provision the preferred arrangement.[6]

8. Provision of recreational facilities

In the Highlands and Islands of Scotland there have been a growing number of examples of a community enterprise being established to provide and run a local swimming pool. Such developments, such as that on the island of Islay, is a partnership between the local community, the District Council, the HIDB (now Highlands and Islands Enterprise) and, in the Islay example, the local distillery. The community raises capital funds, the public and private sectors make grants and donate buildings. The community enterprise runs the pool and ancillary services (cafe, shop, tourist facilities) and receives an annual revenue contribution from the council.

This pattern of provision is becoming the norm in the Highlands and Islands where local councils are simply unable to develop swimming pools themselves. Community run pools are cheaper to operate, partly because of voluntary community input and partly because of greater flexibility - and enthusiasm - to undertake other income-generating activities.

Community provision or management of recreational facilities could become a standard part of the community economy and not just in remote areas. It is surely more appropriate for local people to have control of such local facilities than for them to be contracted out to some private sector leisure industry consortium?

9. Running local tourist/heritage centres

Another example of innovative development, also to be found in the

Highlands and Islands, is the Helmsdale Heritage Centre (Timespan). This is a visitor centre tourist attraction which tells the history of that remote part on the north-east coast of Scotland. It is a collective community effort to build up the number of tourist visits to the town in order to bolster the local economy of shops and guest houses.

The non-profit distributing trust (another name for community enterprise perhaps) is a not uncommon form of structure for other heritage and tourist attractions where local people - or a specialist interest group - preserve a steam railway or develop some other example of local heritage, and endeavour to make it financially sustainable, at least in part, by developing it as a visitor attraction. The Ivanhoe Castle at Conisborough, for example, which is to be re-roofed with City Challenge funds, is run by a consortium of local councils, community representatives and a charity.[7]

10. Providing specialist services to other community enterprises and community organisations

It is important to ensure that the community sector can access sympathetic specialist professional services such as architecture and design, accountancy and legal services and a number of specialist community enterprises have been set up for this purpose.

Other, more established community enterprises have begun to offer consultancy services in their particular area of business expertise. The Allander Group in Glasgow has joined with Community Security in Middlesbrough to offer a consultancy service in establishing security enterprises and estate caretaking. Govan Workspace, in association with its architects, offers a full workspace planning and development service. The North Kensington Amenity Trust has been offering an informal advisory and development service to groups interested in setting up their own Development Trust, anticipating the setting up of the Development Trusts Association.

11. Providing social housing

This is the 'housing sector' of community enterprise comprising, as we saw earlier, community-based housing associations, 'par value' co-operative societies where the co-operators jointly own and manage their homes, and tenant management housing co-operatives where the tenants take a delegated management contract from the local authority (or other) owner of the houses and are responsible for all aspects of management and maintenance, including refurbishment programmes.

The success of these housing initiatives can be quite striking with a very strong sense of community involvement coming from the very direct relationship between involvement and obvious benefit: better housing.

12. **Providing low cost personal loans**

This is the 'finance sector' of community enterprise, the credit unions, which is probably the fastest growing part of the sector. Involvement as a saving member of a credit union is directly linked to benefit as a borrower.

"Touching the life of the community"

A number of general points can be drawn from this listing of community enterprise activities:

First, they tend to be associated with the creation and operation of various 'community infrastructural services', the essential framework within which other small businesses can set up, individuals can gain skills and confidence, commercially marginal services can be sustained, the unemployed can be eased back into the world of work, social and recreational needs can be met through business action. In short they are to do with facilitating integrated economic and social development.

Second, they tend to "touch the life of the community"[8] in that the benefit which accrues from their activity is clearly felt by local people and understood by a significant part of the local community.

Third, there is often a visible physical manifestation of the work of the enterprise with which the local community can identify. Most obviously this can be a building, a 'centre', a major environmental project which local people are working/have worked on, sign-written vehicles going about the area.

Fourth, while some of the activities are potentially self-funding and even profitable, others obviously need some form of continuing financial support. In some cases that can come from profitable commercial activity within the community enterprise group of activities. In other cases that support must come from elsewhere: from the 'sweat equity' of unpaid labour, from revenue grants from the public sector or charitable trusts, or from contracts which recognise the uncommercial nature of the work to be done and are prepared to pay for it.

Fifth, they tend to be activities which are often avoided by the private sector either or both because of poor profit margins (for example island shops and employing the long-term unemployed on landscaping contracts) and/or because of complexity and hassle (multi-use workspace with many tenants on short leases, training tailored to the individual needs of difficult groups). Others are activities from which the public sector is increasingly withdrawing in its, now seemingly out-dated, role of provider.

It is also possible to draw some conclusions about activities which community enterprises are not good at. Attempts have been made to set up as a community enterprise the sort of business more usually run as a sole trader or small partnership: window-cleaning, television repairs, printing, wood-stripping, jobbing joinery...While there has been the occasional success, generally community enterprise has not been successful at running such businesses which are best run by the people working in them, who need to eat and sleep their business as well as work in it, whose rewards must relate directly to the effort they put in. The more appropriate role for the community enterprise is to help local people get it set up, to offer space, to give book-keeping and other support services, rather than run it. This is the role which Bootstrap Enterprises has developed very effectively in Hackney in London: that is, making it possible for local people to set up their own business which may be structured as a worker co-operative or which may be simply a sole trader or a partnership.

There is another reason why it is often impractical for the community enterprise to attempt to run such businesses. Very small businesses operate without VAT registration and to a degree in a cash economy which makes them very 'tax efficient'. By contrast the community enterprise has to be 'squeaky clean' in all its doings and cannot compete with the prices and charge-out rates of businesses able to cross in and out of the black and the white economies.

It is noticeable how seldom community enterprises have become involved in manufacturing in any significant way. In part this is accounted for by the high development costs associated with establishing a manufacturing business and the high cost of setting up a production capacity together with an extended cash flow: community enterprises seldom have had access to such investment levels. But it is also perhaps accounted for by the inappropriateness of the community enterprise model to provide the single-minded drive and determination to set up the business. There is surely some truth in the caricature of the man with an idea, perhaps teaming up with a partner, defying the world to get backing for his project. That is individualistic enterprise unlikely to be found within the setting of community enterprise. Nor does setting up a manufacturing unit "touch the life of the neighbourhood" in the same way as the activities previously described. Again the role of the community enterprise might be to encourage and help, to facilitate but not to do it itself; reinforcing the concept of the community enterprise as local development organisation.

It can therefore be argued that community enterprise should concentrate on those activities which "touch the life of the neighbourhood" and which it has been seen to be good at. It happens that these are activities often eschewed by the private sector and deserted by the public sector. Thus community enterprise can be seen to be filling an important market gap. As well as being appropriate for community enterprise, some of these activities have been seen to be commercially marginal which in turn must temper the commercial expectations we have.

The main argument against accepting this positioning for community enterprise is that it appears to accept a 'second division' status operating in commercially marginal areas.

Multi-layered economy

If we view the world economy as multi-layered and necessarily interdependent, ranging from the trans-national corporation, through national and regional enterprise to small business, the community economy and the household economy, it does not follow that any part is more important than any other, especially as regards contributing to human and planetary well-being. As things stand now, undue power can be seen to be in the hands of the trans-nationals, and to modify that is one of the exciting challenges of which community enterprise is a part: to bring all parts of the world economy under the influence of the values of people-centred development. There will be different ways of achieving that at different layers and community enterprise is one of the appropriate structures for developing and expanding the community economy. It also happens to be operating at what is potentially a most exciting interface, between the informal household and voluntary economies and the formal economy. Thinking in competitive terms of first and second divisions is not appropriate. What is appropriate is relevant structures for identifiable economic tasks.

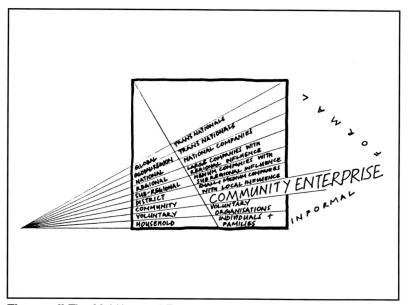

Figure vii The Multi-layered Economy

Figure vii depicts the multi-layered economy. Different enterprise structures operate within and impact at several levels. Thus trans-national and national corporations function over and affect all layers. Small and medium firms will exceptionally operate at national or global regional level, but are very much part of the community economy and affect the household and voluntary layers. Community enterprises will for the most part be part of the district and sub-regional layers. Although they may operate occasionally at 'higher' layers, their operation, influence and impact will mostly be as part of the community economy.

If we accept community enterprise as a relevant structure for the community economy job then we should not ask it to do things for which other structures may be more appropriate. For the most part community enterprise has not been the best way of running thrusting commercial enterprises. Innovative and socially aware structures which have been developed to do that job include Employee Share Ownership Plan Companies (ESOPs), Employee Common Ownership Plan Co-operatives (ECOPs), John Lewis style partnerships, Scott Bader Commonwealths, and it may be that community enterprises will in due course enter joint ventures with such organisations.

An appropriate role

Accepting an appropriate role does not necessarily condemn community enterprises only to unprofitable or unviable activities. Examples such as the Allander Group, Govan Workspace and North Kensington Amenity Trust demonstrate how community enterprises can enjoy commercial success. There will also be occasional examples of a community enterprise setting up a business which hardly touches the life of the neighbourhood but which does make surplus profits which can be recycled into other local activities. For the most part however it is wise for community enterprises to concentrate on what they are good at and on those activities which can be seen to connect directly with community betterment.

The constant aim will be to become financially self-sustaining and to arrange for all payments received for any of its activities to be put onto some form of contract system whereby those purchasing or commissioning a service are clear in advance about what is to be done and what is to be paid for. That can - indeed should - include the community benefit and the community development which derives from the activities of a community enterprise as well the more obvious trading transactions.

The purpose of the finance sector of community enterprise (credit unions) is to offer a service and terms which the banks cannot (nor want to) match. The purpose of the housing sector is to offer special types of affordable housing on terms and conditions which are generally otherwise not available. The purpose of the community businesses, community co-operatives and development trusts should be to concentrate on those parts of the economy which are best tackled with a community focus and dimension.

Community enterprise has generally been associated with areas of disadvantage, poverty, high unemployment and industrial decline. Where there is need, there is always a search for new ways of tackling it. It is likely, and indeed appropriate, that community enterprise will mostly continue to be seen as part of the development 'tool-kit' for local regeneration in disadvantaged areas and funding regimes will continue to be fashioned according to political responses to perceptions of need and potentially successful ways of tackling that need.

Nonetheless the community enterprise concept as a means of developing and expanding the community economy can be equally relevant to better off areas and if we believe that it is desirable that there should be a thriving local economy under community control and predicated on the values of mutual help and common-ownership, then community enterprise should be encouraged to develop in any area. It is not unreasonable however if financial and other support systems are targeted at those communities in greater need. In the better off areas, because the nature of need is different, the starting points are more likely to be areas of social care and recreational provision and such schemes as the successful 'green pound' network in Stroud where members of the network barter their skills and products amongst each other for payment in £stroud: effectively credit against the future provision of goods or a service.

Nor is accepting an appropriate role for community enterprise now giving up on future change in how the economy is to be run. In the long-term it is the values of community enterprise which are important not the detailed organisational structure as it has evolved (and will continue to evolve) to operate within the community economy. As the global economy comes to adopt a new value system, new structures for functions at different layers in the global economy will require to be devised.

Chapter 5

Nature of community

"Each will acquire such irresistible energy in this cause, as no one now comprehends, but which will perpetually keep these societies in the most delightful activity, and afford full scope for all the physical and intellectual powers of our nature."

'Community' in respect of community enterprise has usually been defined in terms of a geographical area, although sometimes a community has been identified as people sharing a common interest or need: for example single-parent families, families with members suffering a particular handicap, players of a particular sport. Where a community of interest is agreed there will also usually be an agreed area of benefit. Although this is likely to be wider than the area associated with a geographically defined community enterprise, it will give a sense of localness to the enterprise. This sense of localness is an important test, for by definition community enterprise requires to be rooted in place as well as in concept. It is this localness, the fact that it cannot get up and go somewhere else, which serves to distinguish community enterprise both from non-local organisations and from other forms of business.

Most community enterprises based on a community of interest or need will have a specific focus and their areas of benefit may well overlap those of other community enterprises. It is also possible that some persons may be members of more than one community of interest enterprise or indeed of a geographically-based enterprise also. These overlapping areas and multiple memberships need pose no problems of conflict (**figure iv**).

The definition of 'community' as applied to spatially-based community enterprises has given rise to continuing debate. Two important lessons can be drawn from the practical experience of the 1970s and 1980s. The first concerns who makes up a community and the second concerns the *optimum community size* for effective development.

A partnership of stake-holders

Much traditional community development starts from the perspective
of a small and localised group of residents in a particular area. Apart
from some remote island and rural areas it is no longer possible simply
to draw a line on a map to designate a 'community'. Modern urban
(and much rural) society is more complex and a geographical
neighbourhood has an infinite number of relationships with other
places, people and institutions which means that it cannot be treated in
isolation. Nor is it realistic to ignore that in any community there are,
besides those who live in it, other 'stake-holders' with a variety of
interests in and responsibilities to the area.

These other stake-holders will include: local or nearby business and
industry; the local authorities and other public sector agencies; various
voluntary and church organisations which operate in the area. True
community development should aim to involve all these stake-holders,
working together in partnership, and developing a common purpose[1]
based on a shared 'vision' for the area. It will not always happen as
comfortably and consensually as that suggests but to attempt
development from the perspective of only one group is both one-sided
and unrealistic. Where that sole group is the local residents working up
their vision alone for the community, it will only be in exceptional
circumstances that they might achieve that vision without the active
help of and input from the other stake-holders.

This is a powerful argument in favour of partnership: genuine
partnership where the stake-holders meet as equals and work together
to agree a common purpose and vision. Too often the development
process starts with residents alone, deciding what they want and then
having to sell the ideas to other bodies; or it starts with one part of the
public sector putting together the multi-agency approach, deciding
what is to be done and seeking community participation (or more
accurately legitimation). In neither scenario is there a sense of
common purpose or common-ownership of the ideas and the plan. In
the former case the local community organisation is likely to spend a
long time struggling with the local authority and others to win a
reluctant consent and the resources for their plans, usually accompanied
by quite stringent controls. In the latter case the multi-agency approach
will go ahead anyway and do what it wants, and on paper it is always
easy to make the structure look as if the community is involved.

Real partnership should mean surrendering the power of decision-
making to the partnership body at community level so that

development planning is genuinely community-led. And in order to ensure that the partnership process works effectively it must allow the local residents access to information, advice and technical help so that they can adequately play their part alongside the other stake-holders. Public and private sector organisations alike must guard against appearing like the 'cavalry coming over the hill' and at the same time be prepared to resource the local community to play its part. In some cases that will mean funding the development role of the core community enterprise (see chapter 3).

Areas and areas

The community enterprise model described earlier operates as a local development agency which might engage both in the direct creation and management of businesses and projects and in the provision of infrastructural facilities to encourage other action which contributes to the growth of the community economy: business management and community development. To do both effectively it will be necessary to achieve a certain size in order to be financially self-sustaining and to operate over an adequately large area. No optimum geographical or population size for a 'viable' area of benefit can be prescribed as it will require to be negotiated and agreed according to local circumstances and according to intended functions. It will vary from urban to rural settings. In a sense this is the notion of 'pragmatic community': one with which people can feel comfortable and which will nonetheless 'work' in the sense of serving its intended purpose. It is possible to isolate some factors which will influence the negotiation of the 'pragmatic community'.

Figure iv illustrated how the area of benefit for differing community enterprise initiatives will vary and overlap. Chapter 4 discussed the complex inter-relations which will evolve in 'real life' community enterprise situations, but concluded that a 'core community enterprise' requires to be identified by sponsors/funders and agreed by local organisations as the recognised local development organisation for an accepted geographical area. Within that area (and indeed overlapping it) there may be a multiplicity of community enterprises operating within the community economy.

To operate on a viable self-sustaining scale the community enterprise, which is acting as a local development organisation (the core community enterprise), must cover a significantly larger area than the small neighbourhoods with which most people immediately identify: a group of villages in a rural district, a small town, a 'bite-sized chunk' of a city, for example, the whole of Easterhouse rather than its 13 local neighbourhoods. It will certainly be bigger than most of the small areas designated for purposes of urban programme funding which can be as small as just a few streets, part of an electoral ward.

In the mid 1980s Strathclyde Community Business used the slogan 'every APT should have one'.[2] That might now be usefully modified to 'every APT should be part of one'. Being part of the area of benefit would give membership rights and access to the benefits of the local core community enterprise.

The activities which were identified in chapter 4 appropriate for a community enterprise to undertake must, in order to be effective as businesses, be set up and run on a scale adequate to their particular requirement. A workspace should really be no smaller than 35,000 square feet and serve a reasonably large area. It does not make sense to set up several small security or landscaping businesses. The economies and effectiveness of scale must be obtained. An effective training programme must be able to recruit trainees and find job opportunities over a sensibly wide area.

The core community enterprise is likely to facilitate the creation of other activities which can and should have a local neighbourhood focus within and smaller than the wider area of benefit: a launderette, a community cafe, a food co-operative. Many such enterprises might be Voluntary Enterprises. The role of the core community enterprise in relation to these enterprises will vary: sometimes it will initiate, sometimes it will respond to a request or a proposal, sometimes the neighbourhood enterprise will be a subsidiary project, sometimes it will become independent but perhaps receive some management help or a book-keeping service, sometimes the community enterprise will manage the neighbourhood project, sometimes not. A similar flexible facilitating relationship could be developed with enterprises structured as worker co-operatives or indeed as traditional small firms. It follows from this that the area of benefit may differ for the various activities undertaken by or through a multi-functional community enterprise.

There need be no conflict between a community enterprise running businesses, projects and services over a sensibly large area and flexibly facilitating or running other neighbourhood-based activities within its wider area of benefit. The key issue is to gain agreement that only one community enterprise will be acting as development organisation within the given wider area.

Convergence of top-down with bottom-up

To achieve that agreement requires a convergence of 'bottom-up' and 'top-down' development strategy and practice. Normal practice has been to start from the bottom up and the consequence is a mosaic of community enterprises, sometimes clustered, sometimes competing with each other for scarce resources and limited markets. A more strategic approach would be to develop a theoretical understanding of how many community enterprises it might be appropriate to support and create in a given region or district and with what area of benefit. Such an approach can only be initiated from the top down, that is by the Training and Enterprise Council (TEC), Local Enterprise Company (LEC) or the council consulting with other parties. That process of consultation must involve at the earliest possible stage local community organisations and groups. It will not be easy but nor will it be impossible for neighbourhood community interests to come to understand the value of being part of a wider community enterprise area of benefit in which there is flexibility to establish neighbourhood enterprises and projects, and the opportunity to play a part in and benefit from larger scale enterprise, training and community service initiatives. Such a strategy will however only have credibility if the strategic planning agencies are seen to be genuinely making a commitment to the development of community enterprise as part of their local development strategy. While the structures to facilitate the emergence of community enterprises may be established to some degree in a 'top-down' manner, the operating structures must be 'bottom-up'.

To those who believe in the purifying value of struggle to achieve a worthwhile community development, the idea of a planned and agreed strategy will be anathema. There is indeed the danger that community enterprise could become co-opted as part of the established way of doing things and dominated by vested interests of the public and private sectors. That is a very real danger and must be safeguarded against by ensuring that the legal structures for community enterprise entrench community ownership of assets and community accountability (see chapter 11) by representative bodies such as Community Business Scotland, Community Enterprise UK and the Development Trusts Association acting as watch-dogs; and by building in the resource capacity for the local resident stake-holders to play their part to the full.

Chapter 6

Human capital

"It is found that when men work together for a common interest, each performs his part more advantageously for himself and for society."

What makes a community enterprise work is the people: the people who have the vision and the enthusiasm to set it up, the people who manage the enterprise, the people who do the work, the people who commit their time and energy to local development. Human capital is the key to success; it is human failings which lead to problems and failure. Indeed some of the persistent difficulties which beset the community enterprise sector are to do with people: undue expectations and inadequate training and preparation.

The role of managers in community enterprises

Effective business management has long been a problem area for community enterprise. It is a particularly difficult task for the manager who finds him/herself between a number of often conflicting demands: market constraints, job expectations of local people, community social objectives, sponsors' requirements, with each faction expecting things to happen much faster than is either realistic or practical.

The position of manager is often an isolated one as few community enterprises are in a position to start with more than one manager. S/he is likely to be an outsider appointed because of her/his skills. There will therefore be a degree of suspicion about 'this stranger', 'this professional' coming into 'our community'. As outsiders, managers will take time to understand the community in which they find themselves and sometimes the culture shock of coming face to face with poverty and deprivation in twentieth century Britain can be considerable.

It is not uncommon for the voluntary board of directors, who have been so active in the planning stages, to 'back off' when 'the professional' arrives, thus exacerbating the feeling of separateness and isolation.

Community enterprises are complex organisations and the task is seldom as simple as running one small business. There will be legal and constitutional complexities. There will be local boards and committees to deal with. There will be local members. There will be bureaucratically complex relations and (dis)agreements with the local council, and probably the county (region) too. There will be local community politics to deal with. There will be helpful and unhelpful support organisations involved. And all of this to deal with before considering the task of actually setting up and running any particular business activity!

The appointment of a manager for a community enterprise, especially in the first instance, is too easily seen as the answer to a range of problems: "if only we had a full-time worker" is the common cry of voluntary committees. Appointments may then be made without a clear job description and without the person appointed being given a 'shopping list' of duties. An analysis of that shopping list might reveal some or all of the following discrete functions:

accountant
administrator
business developer
business manager
community development worker
entrepreneur
fund raiser
market researcher
publicist
sales person

Few people exist who combine the skills and abilities to do all these things; and most of those who might will already be running their own organisation or will be working for a major company or organisation at a salary considerably greater than that on offer by a community enterprise.

Community enterprises and their advisers must be clear about what tasks they require a manager to do and the skills that they are looking for. A distinction should always be made between the generalist management of the community enterprise as local development organisation and the specialist management needs of particular businesses or projects. What is essential is a realistic job description and a realistic person profile to aid in the process of recruitment.

Motivation is much harder to assess, but it is important that persons appointed to management posts within community enterprises at the very least understand the concept, and preferably are enthusiastic about it. While the skills to run any particular business are similar, it is a mistake to claim that a business run by a community enterprise is just like any other: it is not, and there will be times when the essential difference affects day-to-day management.

Salary is a problem. Community enterprises, in common with much of the voluntary sector, expect people to do rather more (in difficult circumstances) for less than they could earn in the private or public sectors. It is unsatisfactory but there is no immediate solution. The ethos of community enterprise would be against the payment of disproportionate salaries and it can be hard for local people living on state benefits to come to terms with paying 'their' manager a salary so far beyond their own comprehension. On the other hand it is important to develop reasonable rates of remuneration and not depend on goodwill.

If community enterprises were accepted as part of the normal 'tool-kit' for local development and if some legislative recognition were to be granted (see chapter 11) then there would be a greater chance of a 'cadre' of community enterprise managers emerging: people who are committed to the ethos and concept of community enterprise and who can make a career within this field. Something of this nature has already been seen within the social housing field; and it is possible to discern the beginnings of similar developments in Scotland with manager transfers between community enterprises and between community enterprises and development units.

Once there is a greater recognition of the community enterprise sector it will become easier to put into place training programmes for community enterprise management: indeed were a National Community Enterprise Agency created (see chapter 11) that body might expect training institutions to prepare appropriate training to meets the needs of the sector. Already some universities include a community enterprise option as part of their MBA course. That could readily be developed into targeted training for a career in community enterprise, with the potential for lateral movement into social housing and into the wider voluntary sector.

Several community enterprises have received management help via secondees from the private sector. The results have been mixed. For the most part management experience in a large company does not fit with the multi-purpose demands of running a community enterprise. The manager used to the resources of his department and all the other departments may not transfer easily to the office on a council housing estate where s/he is all departments in one small room.

An impressionistic analysis of successful community enterprise managers suggests there is no common profile of experience, training or background which leads to success in the job. All seem to be exceptions and come from very different walks in life. There has been no systematic research done, a grave lack which ought to be remedied quickly as all commentators agree that the quality and capability of management has been a key - perhaps the key - factor in determining success or failure.

Another source of potential management talent for community enterprises has sometimes been found amongst the nearly-retired, of whom industrial 'down-sizing' continues to produce a steady stream. There is evidence to suggest that some early retirees, who have their financial security assured, can be interested in a new business career with a social dimension and can afford to do it.

A further important dimension to management training is ensuring that residents from the community enterprise areas and employees within community enterprises can access training to develop management skills. This is what in large organisations would be 'in-house' management development. Few community enterprises are yet big enough to tackle this in any systematic way (although there have been some notable examples of good in-company personal development and promotion). The matter could be addressed through the federal organisations such as Community Business Scotland and the Development Trusts Association.

Management training of this sort requires an investment of funds. Strathclyde Community Business experimented with management training programmes targeted at local community business activists using European Social Fund finance. The results were not encouraging in training people who went on to work in community enterprise management, but were encouraging in the personal and educational development of the individual trainees, the majority of whom moved on positively although outside community enterprise.

The role of boards of directors

Through its constitution the community enterprise provides a means whereby assets can be owned on behalf of ('in trust for') the community and whereby the organisation is accountable to its local constituency either through democratic mass membership or through some other local accountability system.

It has already been established that there is a need to distinguish between the (generalist) management needs of the community enterprise as development organisation and the (particular) management needs of specific businesses or projects. When looking at structure and management at director level it is useful to retain that distinction in mind.

Most community enterprises have adopted a structure whereby particular businesses or projects are run by subsidiary companies, subsidiary to an overall community company, usually based on a local membership. In Scotland where model constitutions have been in use since the early 1980s there are three common structural models (**figure ix**). In England there has been a greater diversity of structure but for the most part those structures used can be interpreted in the context of the Scottish models.

The main purpose of the subsidiary boards should be to run that company effectively within any policy framework handed down from the parent company. In consequence the board of directors should be appointed so as to include the skills needed to do the job in hand. That is likely to include professional and technical competences, but to exclude community representation except where it relates to the actual business itself (for example, tenant representation on a workspace board, consumer representation on a day nursery board). Increasingly these task-oriented boards may include the managers of the business as directors and also worker directors to involve the workforce in the business of management. In chapter 11 we also note the possibility of a workers co-operative linked to a community enterprise.

It should be the parent board of the community enterprise group (the holding company) that ensures communication with and accountability to the local community, where philosophy and social purpose are debated, and from where strategy and new development emerges. A community enterprise which acts as a local development organisation may well have core staff who do development work, while management staff are employed specifically to manage the businesses or other projects that have been set up. The parent board is likely to be larger than the subsidiary boards and to include to a significant degree the representation of community interests.

The Waverley Housing Trust in the Scottish borders has developed this distinction in a particular way. The charitable company, Waverley Trust Ltd, which owns the houses which have been purchased from Scottish Homes, is entirely owned and controlled by the tenants. That company sets overall policy and strategy and sets the rent levels for the houses. The management of the housing however is the job of a separate company, Waverley Housing Management Ltd, which has a three year management contract with the parent company to do a particular job to particular standards. The two companies have one reciprocal member on each other's board, but although linked, they are separate organisations and the management company with its small executive board gets on with the job of managing the houses to the high standard demanded by the Trust.[1] The nature of the contract is such that the Trust can decide not to renew if it is dissatisfied with performance and can offer it to other suitably qualified organisations.

The Allander Group is adopting a different approach more akin to the Scott Bader Commonwealth whereby it will set up a community trust as a forum of wide community interests to which an agreed percentage of profits will be donated each year. The trust will have complete freedom to decide how to use the funds so generated for local community benefit, while the management of the trading companies which comprise the community enterprise group will be managed by much smaller professional and executive boards.

The distinction between the community and development functions on the one hand and business management on the other makes it easier to introduce outsiders into the management of community enterprises at different levels. At community holding company board level it will be useful to introduce people who represent particular local interests or who can offer the community enterprise useful links and valuable introductions. At subsidiary management board level the enterprise will be seeking individuals who may be willing to share their professional expertise in running the actual business or project.

For most local residents, becoming involved in a board of directors and a company is an entirely new experience and one which can easily seem to be daunting. It is therefore important that adequate training is provided both for serving and for potential directors. That training has to demystify companies; at the same time it has to be clearly understood that directors do undertake serious and important responsibilities in the eyes of the law and have to ensure that they are in a position to be able to discharge those responsibilities.

Training has therefore to cover two main themes: the process of running board meetings effectively and the more technical understandings that are required. The first will cover matters like the structure of meetings, effective minutes, the use of sub-committees, chairing, encouraging participation, group dynamics, discouraging domination. The second will deal with understanding accounts, basic employment law, duties and responsibilities of directors etc.

If community enterprise boards are to be truly effective the training process should be ongoing: reflecting and refreshing. Especial care should be taken when a new member joins an established group of directors. Ideally there should be a training course for all new directors. Too often it is just a question of 'turn up and you'll soon get to know us and find out what it's all about'.

For some boards of directors a major problem is their relationship with their manager(s). We have discussed earlier how management problems are the most frequently quoted reason for community enterprise failure. Lay boards are responsible for the appointment of their managers and for overseeing their work, at the same time they are very dependent on them for information and for the professional skills which the board members often do not have. Indeed it has happened that managers are expected to organise training for their own directors.

Where there are professional support agencies, the training of directors has been an important area of work and in more than one case the completion of a basic directors training course has been a pre-condition of receiving financial support.[2]

Charisma and community

Many community enterprises - like other organisations or businesses - are the result of considerable effort, commitment and leadership by one exceptional individual: the product of charismatic energy and determination. Charisma can sit uneasily within a community and democratic structure, often ironically notwithstanding the individual's avowed commitment to the concept of common-ownership. Nor are charismatic innovators always the best people to manage and sustain an organisation once it has been set up.

While this problem of organisation and leadership is not special to community enterprise, it is one which advisers and sponsors must be keenly aware of and ensure that, if innovators have to be challenged or to step down, there is proper support and organisational strength to withstand the inevitable 'wobble' that may ensue. By a similar token they must ensure that the challenge is made, despite discomfort, when it is clear that change is needed.

The difficulties of employing the long-term unemployed

Reference has been made earlier to the important and successful role which community enterprises can play in getting unemployed people back to work. This is an important and practical way in which community enterprises are investing in the human capital of their locality. It is not a simple process and can be seen to consist of three distinct stages:

1. **motivation**: helping people believe again in themselves, in their ability to work and in the value of actually trying to find work. This process was earlier described as 'capacity building' and will include remedial basic skill acquisition such as literacy and numeracy. In short it is to do with helping people, who for various reasons do not feel themselves to be or are not considered to be employable, become capable of work again.

2. getting people back into the **daily routine** of actually working: getting out of bed, getting to work on time, accepting the constraints of routine tasks, regaining physical fitness and mental alertness.

3. placing people in **vocational training** to learn skills relevant to the labour market.

None of these stages can be sensibly achieved within the constraints of a commercially priced contract or working situation. Yet it is important that stage two and the practical aspects of stage three take place in real work situations. (Stages one and two can happen simultaneously as part of the same scheme.) Community enterprises, because they are local and run by local people for local benefit, have demonstrated that they are good at recruiting the long-term unemployed and getting them back to work. They are also able to cope with the sub-cultural pressures which exist in most poor communities because they are part of that same community.

Since the demise of the Community Programme and since the introduction of compulsory competitive tendering, community enterprises have found themselves attempting to achieve stages one and two within the context of commercial contracts. Not surprisingly some have failed in a strict commercial sense and made losses which in some cases have led to winding up the companies concerned. There has seemed to be no way in which the value of their job-creating and training work can be accorded a financial value and paid for. In consequence community enterprises have been forced to back off from areas of work which in the past they have used to employ long-term unemployed people in order to ensure that whatever they undertake is 'commercially sound'.

Government and local government, TECs and LECs must re-assess the way in which the long-term unemployed are targeted, especially at times of rising unemployment. If we are serious about reaching out to them and offering ways of bringing them back into the labour market, then the community enterprise experience should be studied. But there is a price. It is not enough to expect the task to be done as part of a commercially priced contract. The motivating, the back-to-work and the training jobs cost time and money and a sensible method of payment should be devised, most probably based on a per capita weekly fee for an agreed number of weeks, with perhaps some bonus system for successful throughputs into the open labour market. That is something like a cross between Employment Training and Community Programme, permitting community enterprises to employ the long-term unemployed, get them back to work and feed them into vocational training situations or into the open labour market. The corollary of such a scheme would be for public and private sectors to be willing (and permitted by government) to offer special contracts to community enterprises to be used for this job-creating work.

Limits to job creation

The real framework within which all community enterprises are working is one of exceptionally high, and rising, unemployment. Even during the 'Lawson boom' of the middle 1980s the level of unemployment in areas where community enterprises are mostly based stayed high by any standards of historical comparison; few people, the longest and worst affected by unemployment, noticed much change. It is therefore naive to imagine that the labour market will be able to offer the number of jobs required to reduce significantly unemployment levels despite the best endeavours of community enterprise both as job creator and as training organisation. We face a changing situation world-wide where it is quite unlikely that there will always be jobs, as we have known them in the past, for all people who want them, for all the time that they want them.

Community enterprise, a key structure of the community economy, is at the interface of the formal and informal economies, where the counted and the uncounted mingle, where household, neighbourhood and local enterprise intertwine. In an earlier chapter we described a continuum stretching from community business through social enterprise to voluntary enterprise. Perhaps that continuum should extend to include the household economy also.

It would then be appropriate for community enterprise to engage in encouraging and facilitating activities all along the continuum, making the most of the full range of human capital available within the community. Not all those activities will lead to the creation of jobs, but they will add to economic activity in the area: credit unions which provide low interest loans, food co-operatives which provide low cost purchases, voluntary and community cafes which provide cheap meals, 'green pound' schemes which allow the bartering of skills, goods and services. Any economic activity, whether it increases income or reduces costs, has the capacity to improve the quality of life for those affected. More than that, it encourages the growth of skills and confidence and strengthens that store of human capital on which ultimately the future of mankind depends.

Chapter 7

Achieving accountability

"...a meeting shall be held annually in each township...to hear read an official written report prepared by the councils...After the report shall have been read, the meeting shall deliberate and will consider it, and when they have come to a general understanding respecting it, a committee...shall draw up their report on the report of the councils..."

In the classic community enterprise model, accountability is theoretically achieved through the democratic structure based on the old co-operative principles of open membership and one member one vote. Few community enterprises achieve a large membership and all report the dependence of the organisation on a relatively small group who are prepared to be active and to serve on the board of directors or on the management committee. Even where there is a high membership relative to the population - most usually in rural and island communities - there is the same dependence on a small group of activists to keep things going.

Community enterprises are no different from many other community and voluntary organisations in this regard. However it does call into question how far the present arrangements ensure adequate accountability to the community and to the other stake-holders, when a small group of people elected by a small group who turn up at the annual general meeting are held to represent the whole community. Indeed it is not unusual for there to be no election because of a lack of candidates, and for unfilled places on the board to be filled later by co-option. The theoretical model suggests a large and active community membership competing for places on the board. The reality is often very different.

In community action, mass involvement usually occurs only when there is something to challenge or resist: a clear-cut issue where the people know exactly what they want - or do not want. That mass involvement is rarely sustained over long periods of time. Even when interest does remain high and membership levels are sustained, the work devolves onto a small, executive group. That is the only way in which practical work can be done. But it is then easy for the executive group to get out of touch with its constituency, to fail to keep them informed and to cease to be effectively accountable. Often this is not for any sinister reason. It is simply that those involved closely with a project or a campaign forget that others do not have the same means of knowing what is happening as they have.

The membership arrangements in the CBS model constitution are based on the annual renewal of membership. The assumption is that it is better to have a membership which, while perhaps small, has at least re-committed itself each year to being a member and paying the subscription. The annual renewal of membership forces the community enterprise to communicate with its membership once a year. Failure to seek membership renewals energetically will however lead to the gradual reduction of the membership; in some cases reduced to the members of the board only who then become a self-appointing group.

The alternative of membership for life on first joining gives an apparently high membership. This happens in the early days of public meetings and community excitement, but it is a list which rapidly gets out of date through deaths and removals from the district. If there is no regular recruitment campaign the active membership can quickly dwindle to the small self-appointed inner group. The main advantage of the wider membership list however is that papers for the AGM must be sent to all those who appear on it, so the community enterprise must communicate once a year with those members of the community, even if a proportion of the envelopes are 'returned to sender'.

Democracy is a two-way process. People must join and take part. But equally those who run democratic organisations must encourage people to join and participate. It is not enough to have open membership on paper and do nothing to assist people to find out about the organisation and to become involved. It is likewise naive to assume that large numbers of people will want to participate actively in running a community enterprise or that many will make the effort unprompted to come forward. Experience has shown that new activists are best drawn in on a personal basis, and that assumes a willingness on the part of the core group to bring in new people with new ideas who are likely to question and perhaps challenge what is being done.

The open membership of community enterprise must be truly open, and there are a number of strategies which can be employed to ensure that the community is informed and the opportunity is given for people to ask questions and, perhaps, become involved. These strategies will only be as effective as those implementing them want them to be.

First: annual general meetings should be effectively advertised in the local community, at least via the local press and possibly also through posters and leaflets. A requirement to advertise the AGM in the press should be included in the model community enterprise constitution; common practice in the constitutions of many voluntary organisations.

Second: a community enterprise should communicate with its membership - and the local community - at least once in the year in addition to AGM time. Many already circulate a newsletter and this might also usefully be included in the model constitution.

Third: effort needs to be put into recruiting members to the community enterprise. Although a large membership does not necessarily signify better involvement and although the response to recruitment campaigns may be low, it is important that the offer of membership is there and known to be there. Open membership must mean that people can join if they want to and they must constantly be told that. Equally and obversely it is valuable for existing directors and members to be seeking new members and encouraging participation rather than running a closed shop.

Where the community enterprise provides a local service, the users of that service should form an important potential constituency for membership as they have a direct interest in how the enterprise operates. Similarly the employees of subsidiary companies may be members of the holding company and their membership will stem from a direct personal interest.

Fourth: membership of the community enterprise should be recognised in some way. A number of enterprises issue membership cards and this is a useful way of both confirming membership and clarifying what rights a member has and what the aims and objectives of the community enterprise are. It might be useful also for the issue of some form of membership papers to be made a further requirement of the model community enterprise constitution.

Strategies which may be introduced to increase the effective membership of a community enterprise and to ensure that it provides information both to its membership and to its community, only ensure accountability to those who get involved - which may be a fairly small and/or partial group.

Some community enterprise commentators and activists argue that membership is unimportant and that accountability is better achieved in other ways: first, via other representative organisations; second, through 'normal' processes of community lobbying and pressure; and third, by accountability to the local authority as the local democratic elected authority.

In any community there is a range of organisations, each with varying membership. Connection with a number of these can be a good way for a community enterprise to 'root' itself into different parts of the community and establish a bi-lateral flow of information. In this way Govan Workspace has had valuable and effective links with the Govan Fair Committee, the Unemployed Workers Centre, the Community Council, the Rotary Club and the Labour Party. It can be argued that these other organisations will be more successful in recruiting members because of what they do and so the community enterprise can usefully relate to the community through them 'at one remove', rather than to compete for membership. This is especially true in the context of, say, a council housing estate where the tenants association is the main membership organisation.

This surrogate membership can be achieved either or both by admitting local organisations into membership of the community enterprise and allocating places on the board of directors for named organisations. When other organisations nominate directors, care must be taken at the stage of appointing and briefing them to ensure they understand their primary duty as a director will be to the community enterprise and not to the appointing organisation.

One successful community enterprise has openly adopted the structure of a self-appointing trust, arguing that its constitution sets down what it exists for, the trustees will only appoint people with the right 'mind-set' and that if ever the community enterprise went astray in the eyes of the community, there are many local organisations who would exert the necessary pressure via an advisory group and the local authority. In other words they argue that the community enterprise can only operate effectively with the consent and backing of the community and therefore it must retain that. While this arrangement might work in a particular situation it would be dangerous as well as contrary to the fundamental values of community enterprise to advocate such a rejection of democratic principles for general adoption.

The local council is the first effective tier of elective democracy under our present system and as such both the institution and the councillors do in theory represent a legitimate means of accountability to the wider community. In reality their involvement on the boards of community enterprises is more often interpreted as a control mechanism, safeguarding the council's interests, reputation and funds. If community enterprise were to achieve the recognition that has been proposed both legislatively and strategically, then it would be easier for councils to act objectively as a channel of accountability. As the council role changes from being provider to ensurer of provision, community enterprises may no longer be seen to be competing and may become part of the accepted means of achieving development and delivering services, under contract to the council and properly accountable to it.

The lowest elective tier of government, parish and community councils, while relatively unimportant at present in terms of policy development and service provision, can represent a useful legitimating mechanism within a local community and a number of community enterprises offer board seats to their parish or community councils. It may be that future local government re-organisation may offer a greater role to these councils, with their local community enterprise acting as the delivery agent for a range of local services.

Accountability, like democracy, must be worked at: it does not just happen. The democracy of open membership does not necessarily ensure effective accountability to the local community. It is however important as a means of encouraging participation and allowing local people to play an active part in the process of development. That of itself is a fundamental objective of the community enterprise idea: that it should be of the people, by the people. Open membership should therefore remain as a key feature of any recognised community enterprise constitution.

In order to create the right framework for proper accountability, links need to be created with other local organisations (representing both local people and other local stake-holders) and with local elective democracy. The most common working model is to provide for representation at board level, ensuring a balance which will be effective for the functioning of the community enterprise. It is not possible to be prescriptive for all situations but it is possible to assert that accountability can only be achieved through formal and informal links with other organisations and institutions (including the council) in addition to open membership democracy.

Chapter 8

Community enterprise and the public sector

"It ought to be a primary duty of every government that sincerely interests itself in the well-being of its subjects, to provide perpetual employment of real national utility."

The recent history of community enterprise development effectively started with a public sector-led experiment in the Highlands and Islands of Scotland in 1977. The HIDB created a system of support based on encouraging people to do it, funding to help them get started and continuing advice and guidance. That basic support system was adopted and adapted in various ways throughout the rest of Scotland and it is there, north of the border, that we have seen the most concerted programme of community enterprise support in the UK.

That programme has been public sector-led and outwith the Highlands and Islands it has been an alliance between local government and the Scottish Office. Regional development units have been established in eight of the nine Scottish regions, the initiative coming for the most part from the Regional Councils with active participation from some District Councils. The funding regime most commonly used has been the urban programme with 75% coming from the Scottish Office. Over the years this public sector 'leadership' has been 'encouraged' by considerable pressure from the grass-roots of the community enterprise movement, largely through its federation Community Business Scotland. This was especially so during the first half of the 1980s when CBS campaigned strenuously - and successfully - for the establishment of development units throughout Scotland.

The early community enterprise programme emanated from the social strategy sections of local authority. More recently established units are likely to be linked to economic development departments. The significance and implication of this shift has been discussed elsewhere: it does not represent the fusion of social and economic development which community enterprise protagonists have argued for but a shift during the decade of the enterprise culture to perceiving the desired outcome of community enterprise to be business development as distinct from community development.

Scotland v England

In England and Wales there has not been anything like the same support network for community enterprise as in Scotland and the nature of support available varies according to local authority. The Welsh Development Agency has created a small community enterprise section but it does not amount to a comprehensive support scheme such as the regional units in Scotland. There are probably four factors which have contributed to the difference in arrangements north of the border.

First, Scotland is a smaller country (by population) with good informal and formal networks of communication and good links, despite political differences, between local government and Scottish Office bureaucracy. Second, there has been no effective community enterprise federation serving England and Wales in the same way that Community Business Scotland has served Scotland. Third, the Department of the Environment, has been until recently much more reticent than Scottish Office colleagues in the Urban Renewal Unit about using the urban programme for local economic development and in particular for community enterprise. Fourth, it has been possible in Scotland to develop an agreed model legal structure for a community enterprise holding company which is acceptable as a charity.

By contrast it is worth noting that both north and south of the border there has been steadily increasing public sector support for credit union development agencies, many of which are funded via the urban programme. Also, by contrast, the community-based social housing movement of housing associations and co-operatives receives funding and other assistance from the public sector as a consequence of the roles which have been identified for them both in national and local strategies.

Separate development

In Scotland community enterprise development units have been set up as 'arm's-length' organisations, companies independent of the local authority. Although in theory independent, in practice the development units have found themselves to be very much under the control of their main funders, the local authorities. Indeed some have argued that the spurious independence has achieved the worst of two worlds. On the one hand they are in effect controlled and must do as directed yet on the other there is a sense that community enterprise has been marginalised. It is separate from the council, part of the voluntary sector; the annual grant to the Development Unit becomes the sum total of local authority interest in and concern about community enterprise.

In Strathclyde this was evidenced in a very striking way: community enterprises found that if they were in receipt of financial help from the development unit they could not qualify for other standard support for small businesses provided by the council. This contrasted with the Highlands and Islands where the arrangement of specialist support was designed to establish a 'level playing field' so that community enterprises could access the normal range of grants and loans available to small firms generally.

The 'apartheid phenomenon' of separate development has probably led to a diminishing of mutual understanding. Local government members and officials move on electorally or for career development and those who initially advocated support for a particular programme such as community enterprise are not always there when the question comes up for reconsideration after the passage of time. The community enterprise development unit, disconnected from the local authority and with funding secure for a number of years, gets on with the job as it perceives it and inevitably evolves its own traditions and thinking. Once a programme is no longer new, members and officials alike can quickly lose interest in favour of the next new scheme. Separate development means that neither side knows what the other thinks it is doing and that ignorance is exacerbated if strenuous efforts are not made to keep people in touch and, more importantly, on side. It is a fact of life also that it falls to the separate smaller body to make the running as regards communication and in Scotland the community enterprise movement was not always as conscious as it might have been of the need to communicate.

Funded but not accepted

One particular consequence - and an especial paradox - of separate development was that despite community enterprise having been funded in Scotland by local and central government, it has never become an accepted part of local development strategy as evolved by the public sector during the 1980s. A contributory factor to this paradox must be the uncertainty within the public sector about where to 'fit' community enterprise: is it part of social strategy, or is it part of economic strategy?

There is little evidence to suggest that the public sector has examined results in order to learn lessons for replication and come to a strategic view about the role the community enterprise model might play in the process of regeneration. The general policy appears to be more the laissez-faire one that if a community decides they would like to try to set up a community enterprise then there is a support organisation to which they can turn for assistance. There is no sense of the public sector having thought through the role that community enterprise might play and then positively encouraging that as part of the local development strategy.

One of Scotland's most successful community enterprises is a managed workspace. The first property which it developed was a disused primary school. That development was backed, after a struggle, by the regional council with urban aid grants, both capital and revenue. The district council joined in as did various trusts and private companies including British Shipbuilders and Shell UK. ERDF grant was awarded. The workspace pioneered not only the concept of small managed workspace in Scotland but also the use of old schools for industrial, job-creating purposes at a time when both ideas were virtually unknown, unfashionable and greeted with considerable scepticism by the prevailing wisdoms of industrial and property development.

The story of the workspace is of steady growth and expansion and of making a significant contribution to job creation and economic regeneration in a part of the city which had been most severely affected by the decline in ship-building on the Clyde and the recession of the 1970s. The community enterprise now manages more than 140,000 square feet of workspace on three sites.

The local authority played a key role in initiating and supporting the workspace. Instead of applauding its success and its own role in it, the council proceeded to spend nearly seven years in bitter wrangle with the company over the terms of the lease of the primary school, arguing at one point that a fully commercial rent should be charged based on the value of the buildings as improved by the community enterprise. The wrangle was only resolved in 1991 when a purchase price was finally agreed.

In the intervening period many schools had been closed down and many workspace projects had been developed in the region. At no point does it appear that the local authority considered replicating the community enterprise model which was working so well. Why? In fact the council joined a partnership with other public and private sector interests to set up another local regeneration agency in the area, part of whose remit was to increase workspace provision: in direct competition with the community enterprise.

The manager of another highly successful community enterprise reports its continuing inability to persuade a key local authority to 'tweak' its procurement and contracting practices to at least give his company a chance of competing for work. Yet it was the same council that initially funded the creation of the community enterprise.

Islands of success

Looking around the country one sees examples of undeniable success: North Kensington, Coin Street, Vauxhall, Glasgow, Loftus, Papa Westray. One is left wondering why the formula is not being repeated again and again. These are still exceptions; and from the community level the talk is of the constant frustration and anguish of having to struggle and fight to win support and credibility.

There is a school of thought which believes that no development is worthwhile unless it is achieved after a struggle. Such thinking condemns new ideas to remain on the margins when the real task is to overwhelm conventional thinking and create a new convention. For community enterprise it means trying to answer some of the 'why' questions which are resulting in local development opportunities being lost.

The growth of community enterprise, in Scotland especially, received political and bureaucratic support from a number of key individuals. However that support did not convert into a general political support at either local or national level and individual support can be extremely volatile within elective institutions.

In his book about Govan Workspace, Buchanan records a senior council official as commenting: "I'm not sure whether support for it (community enterprise) has grown so much as the opposition has decreased".[1] While in their 1992 feasibility study the DTA reports: "A failure by local authorities to accept or understand the potential role of development trusts was of concern to some of those interviewed, as was local authority bureaucracy which was felt by some to be a system which militates against partnership thinking, the fundamental ethos behind the work of development trusts".[2] By similar token the Pandora's Box column in the May/June 1992 issue of *New Sector*[3] (**figure viii**) reinforces that feeling of frustration felt by community enterprise activists when anticipated support from local government does not materialise.

Rotten Borough Council has declared the unmitigated success of its community enterprise development strategy. So successful has it been that it now intends to wind up its community enterprise development unit and redeploy its resources into its new "We're Proud of Rotten" division which will build on the Council's economic achievements by generating civic pride in Rotten's inhabitants.

Rotten's success story began in the mid 1980's when a trip by Councillors to the Scottish region of Strathtay proved an eye-opening experience. Strathtay had developed nearly 50 community businesses through its development unit employing 35 members of staff and with a budget of £2 million per annum. On returning from Strathtay, Rotten's Councillors immediately passed a resolution re-designating one of their officers as Community Enterprise Development Officer (C.E.D.O.) and setting a five-year target for the achievement of results on a par with Strathtay. All this was to be achieved on a "no cost" basis to the Council.

Enthusiastic

Rotten's Community Enterprise Development Officer was enthusiastic. He threw himself into the task of making Rotten's inner city areas and outer estates prosperous again through the efforts of the local residents. Evidence of his efforts was soon apparent. Officials of the Department of Transport ordered an urgent enquiry into the grooves cut into the M6 by over-loaded coaches of Scottish consultants travelling in one direction passing unemployed Rotten residents going the other way. Soon the Government was found to finance these mutual exchanges providing a much needed boost to the inter-dependent industries of Scottish community business consultants and English coach companies. Rotten's C.E.D.O. even found resources to train community business activists.

All this activity was bound to achieve results. Within a year, Rotten's reputation as a forward thinking local authority, dedicated to the welfare of its poorest inhabitants, had won it accolades. At a national conference held in Rotten Town Hall, the Chairperson of the Council's Economic and Community Affairs Committee was able to point to the successes of Rotten's strategy in increasing the confidence of the Borough's residents. A succession of local unemployed activitists then took the platform to prove the point.

Encouraged

It was shortly after this event, however, that matters began to take a different turn. First one, then another, of Rotten's developing community enterprise steering groups completed their period of training and looked for resources to launch their community business. Encouraged and nurtured by the council, they now had solid business plans backed up by extensive research and with significant support in their local communities. Now, however, they needed capital and the council was not prepared for that eventuality.

Within weeks, Rotten's Community Enterprise Development Strategy was in ruins. At first the Council Finance Officers referred the groups to Government sources, but nothing was doing there. A multitude of other agencies was tried, but the answer was always "we can't help you unless you get your Council's support first". "But we have got the Council's support; they told us about community enterprise, they trained us, and they helped us write our business plans," replied the groups. The funding agencies were uninterested, nevertheless, arguing that the local authority could not have much faith in the business plans if they were not prepared to invest themselves.

Rotten Borough Council's Community Enterprise Development Officer now found himself isolated within the Council. No matter how he tried to point to the strategy documents and policy commitments which provided the rationale for his work, he could not escape the blame for creating demands the Council was not prepared to meet. He pointed to the milions of pounds invested in Scottish community businesses and reminded Rotten's Councillors of their visit to Strathtay. But no, Rotten's Councillors were not prepared to divert a few thousand pounds from their multi-million pound efforts to attract Japanese companies to Rotten, and that was the end of it. Worse still, Rotten's Councillors were finding discontented residents attending their surgeries to complain about the funding crisis, in areas where they had previously been quiet and compliant (but poor).

Then, one day, the C.E.D.O. found an official-looking brown envelope on his desk. It contained a letter from the leader of the Council. This letter had to be read twice, and its contents were difficult to believe. After so long in conflict with his employers, after many threats to his job, our C.E.D.O. was being offered an increase in salary, management responsibility and the chance to shape Council policy through a whole new unit, the "We're Proud of Rotten" division. Inset is the final paragraph of the letter.

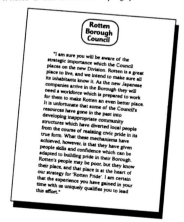

Rotten Borough Council

"I am sure you will be aware of the strategic importance which the Council places on the new Division. Rotten is a great place to live, and we intend to make sure all its inhabitants know it. As the new Japanese companies arrive in the Borough they will need a workforce which is prepared to work for them to make Rotten an even better place. It is unfortunate that some of the Council's resources have gone in the past into developing inappropriate community structures which have diverted local people from the course of realising civic pride in its true form. What these mechanisms have achieved, however, is that they have given people skills and confidence which can be adapted to building pride in their Borough. Rotten's people may be poor, but they know their place, and that place is at the heart of our strategy for 'Rotten Pride'. I am certain that the experience you have gained in your time with us uniquely qualifies you to lead this effort."

Did he take the job? Well, would you?

Figure viii Extract from *New Sector*

Local government has been under increasing assault during the period of the conservative administrations since 1979 and that assault has been slowly but effectively eroding local government power and its freedom of operation. In a sense community enterprise is also about eroding local government power for it is about delegating; relinquishing certain tasks to community structures; allowing communities to take both power and responsibilities. Thus community enterprises can be perceived as a threat and as 'siding' with central government in the context of the present state of relations between central and local government.

The issue of contracting out services is but one good example. Local communities have known for years that local government provision of services has not been of the highest quality, giving rise to frequent complaints from tenant and resident organisations. Local communities have longed claimed the right to 'do it for ourselves' and have not necessarily opposed the principle of contracting out certain services. Ironically few community enterprises have so far been able to win contracted-out contracts, largely because they have been specified in such a way that community enterprises cannot consider tendering. Instead of community enterprises being encouraged they have been more often 'warned off', almost as if privatised services are seen as preferable to services under community control.

Subsidiarity

Community enterprise in the sense that has been developed in previous chapters is a mechanism for undertaking a range of local tasks, mixing the commercial with the social, the profitable with the non-profitable, but operating always within the framework of the market and within the parameters of business efficiency. It could be that community enterprise could replace local government as the main providers of certain services at community level, as for example we have begun to see with swimming pools in the Highlands and Islands. Even to articulate that gives rise to a growing anxiety within a local government structure facing inevitable change and under continuous threat of powers and responsibilities being diminished. Nevertheless maybe the impending re-organisation of local government gives an opportunity to re-assess creatively the role of community enterprise as provider at the community level but within an enabling framework of reorganised local government. The trend towards locally managed schools, hospitals and other services has already been established and it derives from the same principle of subsidiarity which argues in favour of community enterprise playing a larger role in respect of community service provision. The problem - and this is the fundamental issue with regard to the present government's policy - is when the overriding criterion for judging success and performance is a financial one and where the driving motivation appears to be more about cutting costs than improving quality. This is a point to which we return in a later chapter on community benefit auditing.

Political or bureaucratic support

The nearest the community enterprise movement came to achieving significant political support was probably in 1980 when Jim Prior and his deputy at the Department of Employment gave serious consideration to adjusting the Special Temporary Employment Programme (STEP) in such a way as it would, in part at least, be targeted at helping unemployed people set up community enterprises, trading in the market place alongside other small businesses, instead of just being a job creation scheme of community good works.[4] In fact all that happened was the adoption of the name Community Enterprise Scheme but not the substance.

Judging by the party political manifestos at the time of the 1992 general election, community enterprise simply does not feature in any significant way as part of the local development strategy of any of the main parties.

Central government support for community enterprise has been strongest in Scotland through the HIDB and through the Scottish Office's commitment of urban aid. When the Scottish Enterprise legislation was before Parliament, Tony Worthington MP was successful in winning an amendment which gives Scottish Enterprise the duty to support community enterprise.[5] In 1991 Scottish Enterprise made a modest three year grant to Community Business Scotland.

In England the DOE has tended to be less enthusiastic about committing urban programme funding to community enterprise but there is firm evidence to suggest that is now changing. During 1991 the Department financially assisted the BITC Investing in Community Enterprise Initiative and the feasibility study into the setting up of the Development Trusts Association. Both these commitments and the eventual decision to grant-aid the Development Trusts Association in August 1992 are suggestive of a growing interest in the idea, as has been the significant DOE support for some major development trust initiatives such as the one in Manchester's Moss Side.[6]

Partnership and local action

Generally, development policy of recent years has been characterised by 'partnership', for the most part between the private and public sectors. Government has been at pains to bring the private sector more into the local development process, especially employment and training. The TECs and the LECs are evidence of the increased role which is being desired of the private sector; City Challenge, Task Force and the like illustrate the partnership approach. While 'community representatives' are frequently invited to participate in these partnerships, the sense is that they are top-down multi-agency approaches where the community is involved "to grease the wheels of implementation" rather than truly effective partnerships of equals, starting from a bottom-up analysis of need leading to an agreed agenda for action: partnerships which change the way decisions are made and effectively give away an element of power to the local level.

In the 1960s Harold Wilson's government set out to do away with poverty by tackling the remaining 'persistent pockets' in a few small areas by adopting a multi-agency approach to service provision with community participation. What the national Community Development Projects[7] told us was that poverty, far from being eradicated, was growing fast and that economic and structural forces far outside local communities were responsible for poverty and inequality, for squalor and disadvantage. Thirty years and a succession of small area initiatives on, the extent of poverty in Britain has worsened and it is clear that local control over the forces that influence what happens is even more slender.

That is not to deny the relevance of the small area approach where it genuinely is local action within an understood global context. But it only makes sense if it really is on the basis of those with a stake in the area being empowered to decide themselves what should be done, how and when. That is the principle of subsidiarity in action: the concept with which we have recently become familiar and which Cassell's 1992 *Concise English Dictionary* defines as "the principle in government that decisions should wherever possible be taken at the lowest, or most local, level".

Within the multi-layered framework, starting with the household economy and stretching via the community economy to national and on to global level, there will always be debate about what should be done at which level. Local communities, as with nation states, will always want to draw more decision-making and action down to their level than local government or the EC, for example, will be keen to give up. There will be ebbs and flows of power between levels: that is natural. But the essential framework which must be willingly endorsed first must be subsidiarity: handing down the power to decide, and when the power is handed down it must be in an absolute and genuine fashion. Subsidiarity is not about participation but about the real delegation of power, and the responsibility which accompanies it.

All public sector activity is bedevilled by what can only be described as 'short-termism', dictated largely by the ballot box and, increasingly, opinion polls. Too often new initiatives are announced to gain a certain position and then are forgotten until another impetus is required: and impetus is seldom achieved by referring back to old ideas. That this is the way of things may explain but it cannot excuse. Local development is a serious matter which requires long-term stability of purpose. It cannot sensibly be done through a series of (usually) three year initiatives. Investment in business is done on a much longer-term scale. Community investment should be equally long-term.

Chapter 9

Community enterprise and the private sector

"A country can never be beneficially wealthy while it supports a large portion of the working classes in idle poverty or in useless occupation."

'act global, think local'

The jingoist western response to the collapse of the Soviet empire suggesting that capitalism had 'won' the cold war was as distasteful as it was naive. The eastern block system has indeed been totally discredited both as a totalitarian political system and as a centrally planned economic system, both of which had signally failed to work, leaving in their wake a sad trail of environmental degradation, human rights abuse and collapsing economies. It is however as false to deduce from the collapse of the communist bloc that the socialist ideals which were so distorted by the perverse ways in which they were applied and implemented have failed as it is to claim that the opposing capitalist values have succeeded. The western capitalist economic machine is clearly unable to cope with and tackle the important issues which face the world, in particular poverty, the environment and escalating wars.

For those who take a more balanced view of the world than the jingoists, the search is on for ways in which the capitalist economy and the institutions which make it up can be modified so as to serve the people and the planet. There is no argument about the fact that the communist system has been shown to have failed, but equally there is no valid claim either that capitalism has 'won'. The world requires an economic system which works for the benefit of all and that in turn means that private business - international, national and local - has to face up to an awesome responsibility.

In his book *Future Wealth*[1] James Robertson describes how "the centres of medieval cities were dominated by cathedrals; today's cities are dominated by the tower blocks of international banks" symbolising the way in which it seems as if the economy is god and the people of the planets mere pawns to worship in the cathedral banks and make the sacrifices that are needed to appease the god economy: in the process helping its acolytes become rich and powerful.

Business and finance operate across the globe and are way ahead of the political and social institutions not only in understanding the globalisation of affairs but also, and more importantly, in being able to act globally. That global perspective has tended to ignore understanding of or sensitivity to the local contexts which represent 'their world' for most people and of the impact international business and finance has on those local worlds. However there are pressures emerging which can be seen to be pushing towards adopting the obverse of Gandhi's dictum: 'act global, think local'.

It is not in the interest of business that large numbers of the world live in abject poverty: they have little value as a 'market'. In the richer nations, large numbers of poor and disadvantaged unemployed likewise are poor markets and the tinder-box for the conflagration of social unrest. Yet business finds itself able through technological advances to manage with fewer and fewer employees. These and other factors are pushing business (for reasons of self interest) to understand better the wider context within which they operate and the consequences of their actions on other groups in society. As communities become more environmentally sensitive, companies come to recognise that they must win and retain a 'licence to operate', by which they mean the consent of the local community. Companies, when 'down-sizing', are devoting increasing resources into counselling the prospective unemployed and arranging programmes of retraining.

Stake-holders

The idea of different 'stake-holders' in business has been established for some time, recognising that groups other than the share-holders have an interest in the success or failure of a company and therefore should have certain rights of accountability: employees, the local community, customers. The stake-holder idea has been broadened to include the notion of business itself as a stake-holder in society, with responsibilities and duties to the wider community; in some ways a reversion to the nineteenth century ideas of industrial philanthropy when the captains of industry really were part of the local community and played active roles in municipal affairs as well as in charitable and welfare activities, a tradition which has perhaps persisted more firmly in the United States than it has in Britain. This is often referred to as Corporate Community Involvement (CCI). At its best it is about a company playing a full and active role in the local, national and world community, understanding the impact its actions will have and endeavouring to ensure that what it does will produce common good. At its cynical worst it is about public relations.[2]

It is possible to discern a three stage trend in CCI thinking: starting with the public relations perspective; moving on to beginning to understand the corporate self-interest of operating in viable, orderly and safe local communities; to accepting full responsibility to act as good corporate citizens, stake-holders with others in the community with a common concern for mutual welfare.

This idea of corporate social responsibility suggests that business has a moral responsibility to function for the benefit of humanity rather than just for the benefit of share-holders. It is a view ecumenically endorsed in his 1991 *Encyclical* by Pope John Paul: "The purpose of a business firm is not simply to make a profit...other human and moral factors must be considered which are at least equally important in the life of business"[3] and by the Archbishop of Canterbury who has "questioned whether industry was fulfilling its purpose when prolonged bouts of private sector-led growth left more people than ever hungry, thirsty, ill, naked or in prison". The purpose of industry, he suggested, was to create goods and services to meet the community's needs "not to make money for its own sake".[4]

This thinking has also received the 'royal assent'. Speaking in Davos during 1991 Prince Charles is reported as having gone even further when "he appealed to business leaders to stop being preoccupied with short-term profits and instead take the lead in building a world which addressed more basic human needs than balance sheet totals".[5]

This view of capitalism accepts that the world needs the institutions of trans-national business and finance but argues that these institutions should modify their traditional objectives. Instead of being responsible to share-holders, they should recognise and act upon their responsibilities to the planet, to the population of the world, to those who work for them and to the local communities in which they are particularly active. In other words it suggests that the value base of capitalism should be modified to embrace working for the common good of all those factions: the stake-holders in the world. It suggests that it is not impossible to achieve profits for share-holders and to benefit the community without prejudice in either direction because ultimately it is in the interests of business and finance not to ignore what is happening to the planet and its people.

Changing value base

It takes the long-term rather than the short-term perspective. Furthermore a moral position has been introduced. There is a choice. The Archbishop, Pope and HRH are each saying that 'profit' and 'balance sheet outcomes' are not the only measurement: other measurements may be more important.

Changes to the value base of capitalism can come by way of voluntary adoption of new standards and can be legislated for by national governments or by supra-national organisations. Both methods are currently happening and despite the world-wide rhetoric about market forces there is growing evidence within business itself that other new factors must be considered.

The Valdez principles[6] which have been adopted by a number of US companies to regulate their environmental policies and practice are a good example of voluntary regulation. The Community Re-investment Legislation[7] in the US is a good example of how legislation can be used, in this case forcing banks to reinvest in their local community. The climate change and bio-diversity conventions agreed at the Rio summit in June 1992 are examples of modest international agreement and steps which might lead to real and effective measures in due course. New Consumer[8] based in the north-east of England is an organisation dedicated to mobilising the power of the consumer to influence the practices of large manufacturing companies and multiple retailing chains by providing carefully researched information to demonstrate just what impact these organisations have on the planet and its people. Their approach is to achieve social change by consumers (the people) influencing and working with companies: capitalism under community influence, if not control.

Michael Meacher, a Labour front bench spokesman, has written: "The issue is therefore no longer capitalism versus old-style socialism, but a capitalist market economy versus a socialist market economy. Both have an interest in market freedoms, disciplines of efficiency and competitiveness and entrepreneurial innovation".[9] There is a surprising common ground emerging which as little as five years ago would not have seemed likely. Business efficiency and discipline, and competition are accepted as sensible ways of doing things in contrast to central bureaucratic planning. But wider responsibilities have come onto the agenda which must inevitably modify market freedoms, not least the changing value base which questions the primacy of return on investment for share-holders as the key criterion for measurement.

Involvement in community enterprise

At community level, private sector involvement in community enterprise has been modest compared to public sector involvement. Nonetheless various community affairs departments have provided financial assistance, technical help and secondees for a wide range of community enterprise initiatives throughout the country. In the initial stages of the development of Govan Workspace, for example, small grants from British Shipbuilders, Shell UK and the National Westminster Bank enabled the local organisation to maintain momentum in its planning and in its negotiations with the public sector. A commonly reported and applauded characteristic of private sector financial support is that decisions are usually made swiftly, in contrast to the more ponderous processes of the public sector. British Petroleum has had a long involvement with community enterprise, having been involved in a very early study, *Whose Business is Business?*[10] designed to convince Government to back the community enterprise concept via the Manpower Services Commission, and having provided financial and other support for such varied initiatives as West Calder Community Holdings, the publication of *CB News*[11] and most recently the formation of a community enterprise support unit in the south-west of England: Bristol and Avon Community Enterprise Network (BACEN).

Much private sector support for community enterprise has been co-ordinated via Business in the Community (BITC)[12] and the Action Resource Centre (ARC), although the community affairs departments of large companies generally prefer to make their own arrangements with the projects they consider assisting. The Investing in Community Enterprise initiative of BITC (see chapter 10) demonstrated a considerable interest within the business and finance sectors to become involved in community enterprise. This growing commitment to and understanding of the community economy is confirmed by a number of commentators and indicative of the considerable change since an official of the Scottish Development Agency explained how the Agency could do little in a place like Easterhouse "because it has no economy".[13]

Good corporate citizenship

It is argued elsewhere that community enterprise should ideally be the product of a genuine partnership of community stake-holders led by the local community residents but, including the private sector as good corporate citizens. It is also argued that community enterprise is a particular type of organisation especially appropriate to operating within the community economy and providing services which are best organised at local level and which, for differing reasons, both private and public sectors are unlikely to provide in the future. The case is made for legislatively recognising the 'difference' of community enterprise from other forms of business and for consequential positive discrimination in favour of it from both public and private sectors.

Taken together this creates the framework within which the private sector might be expected to become more actively involved in community enterprise: as corporate citizens rather than as profit-seeking companies, creating enterprises which are for the most part not competing in the mainstream of competitive markets but playing an essential part in keeping the community economy healthy and maintaining a high standard of local services. Corporate involvement will not be undertaken with the expectation of obtaining the normal rate of return on investment, but to fulfil obligations of social responsibility. The fulfilment of those obligations is for the present voluntary. For the future a strong case can be made for society, via 'carrot' systems and codes of practice, to ensure that current best practice becomes the norm.

People power

It is also helpful to make a distinction between the overall economic system within which the private sector - and indeed all of us - operates and the people who make the bits of the system work at various levels. It is easy from a community perspective to be so deeply suspicious of 'the system' that the potential for change from within is overlooked. Yet the greatest realistic potential for change lies with those many individuals working as part of the 'private sector' who believe that the traditional value base should change and who are deeply concerned about poverty, about the degradation of the planet and believe that the private sector has got to play a very different role according to very different rules in the future if the world is to survive and provide a satisfactory life for the next generations of inhabitants.

Chapter 10

Investing in community enterprise

"The rich and the poor, the governors and the governed, have really but one interest."

During 1991 Business in the Community ran an initiative called Investing in Community Enterprise. The main purpose of this initiative was to examine the investment needs of community enterprise and to explore how the normal private sector might meet them. The initiative successfully brought together a wide-ranging group of community enterprise practitioners, support organisations, government departments, local authorities, private businesses and financial institutions. An initial two day seminar in July led to a six month participative study and a recall conference held in February 1992.[1]

The initiative identified examples of successful community enterprise where there is clear evidence of the local impact, evidence which convinced participants who had not before had dealings with community enterprise that the concept might be sound. It was also an easy matter to demonstrate the need for finance: you cannot revitalise the Vauxhall area of Liverpool without committing investment. The Coin Street site in Waterloo is a valuable asset but to convert it from car park to living community requires finance.

The problem emerged when the initiative moved on to discuss how the financial sector might invest in community enterprise projects and on what terms. At this point a clash of culture and values became apparent. Community enterprise development is fundamentally about the eventual community benefit. Private sector investment is more about maximising financial return on investment. Thus private finance can be available to invest in community enterprise provided that it can offer the proper rate of return on that investment. Because the risks involved are perceived to be greater, the ultimate return will have to be greater: high risk equals higher return. Higher return drives a development in particular directions; in Coin Street for example it would have seen office blocks whereas Coin Street Community Builders wanted (and have got) houses for local people. Community enterprises of all types, because of what they are, where they are and what they want to do, are unlikely to be 'good' investments viewed from a traditional standpoint.

The discussion then centred on whether an investment vehicle (ie fund) could be established which by various strategems would make it possible for private finance to achieve its optimum rate of return: it was never on the agenda that maybe the rate of return and therefore the actual purpose of investment should be questioned. The strategems proposed included:

1. the portfolio approach to allow the fund to offset some (few) high performance community investments against others which perform more to the community enterprise norm.

2. seeking gift finance from the community support programmes of the private sector to help capitalise the fund and permit 'poor' return investment to be made.

3. seeking various 'tax breaks' and fiscal incentives from government which in essence amount to a public sector subsidy to ensure that the 'proper' rate of return on investment can be paid to private investors.

The holding of this debate is progress because it begins to signal recognition that both public and private sector finance might be invested in community enterprise initiatives, in reasonably significant sums. And without some mechanism to release significant sums, community enterprise will be kept at the margins, generally only able to promote small schemes and only exceptionally to assemble the sorts of package which might replicate a North Kensington Amenity Trust.

In parallel with the creation of a 'mechanism', community enterprises must ensure that structures are in place to permit them to receive equity investment as well as or instead of loans. The share company subsidiaries of the Scottish legal structure model (**figure ix**) were designed partly with the injection of external equity in mind. In any example of such investment however there will need to be strict controls to ensure that the ultimate control of the business does not slip away from the hands of the community holding company.

£30,000 companies

The most systematic funding systems which have been created for community enterprise in Britain are to be found in Scotland. The original scheme of the HIDB launched in 1977 served as a model and was to a degree replicated first in Strathclyde and then in the other regions of Scotland. The HIDB scheme was appropriate on the whole for the scale of business in the scattered and remote communities of the west and north of Scotland. The scheme as developed in lowland Scotland evidenced a number of drawbacks.

First, a significant part of the funding available was revenue grant to pay for a manager and administrative support and this grant could be annually renewable for up to seven years. While it is comforting to have funds secured for a manager in this way, starting up a business on the basis of revenue grant paid in quarterly instalments is both inappropriate and unwise. What is needed is investment and working capital, not the false security of a regular revenue grant cheque.

Second, the £30,000 syndrome took hold. This was the maximum revenue grant available (agreed in 1984) and was also the maximum capital grant for specific items of equipment. In consequence nearly all community enterprises that were set up were '£30,000 companies': the availability of funding dictated size and shape rather than carefully worked out proposals.

A third and final drawback which is most obvious with the benefit of hindsight was the failure to distinguish between development work and business management; and to understand that while the latter could (and should) be met eventually from trading it was unlikely that the former could be, except in the very long-term or in very exceptional circumstances.

The funding regimes in Scotland have tended to dictate that small, undercapitalised businesses were created, too dependent on revenue grant from urban aid, from Community Programme and from ESF projects.

It was this pattern of funding and the lack of investment capital which led to the formation and launch in 1989 of the Scottish Community Enterprise Investment Fund (SCEIF). Aiming to raise £1m of preference shares, SCEIF in fact raised £250,000. While this was not an uncreditable achievement, it did nothing to lift community enterprise investment out of the small scale. Consequently SCEIF, along with some of the Scottish Development Units, finds itself unable to invest all the funds it has available. It is a paradox, but because the funds available are modest, only modest schemes can be considered: and it will not be modest schemes that will make significant regeneration impacts in poor communities.

Social investment

What was innovative about SCEIF was its approach to the 'social investor'; the person who is concerned about what their money is used for rather than the extent of return to themselves. Within the past decade a growing number of social investment opportunities have opened up: offers to buy preference shares in Traidcraft plc, the importer of Third World goods based in Newcastle; a share launch by Industrial Common Ownership Finance Ltd, the national loan fund for workers co-operatives; Shared Interest, a social investment fund specialising in overseas projects. The largest of all social investment organisations is Mercury Provident plc which is effectively an alternative bank, safeguarding depositors and investors money, offering limited return on investment and investing only in socially and environmentally sound projects and enterprises.[2]

A continued growth in social investment through Mercury, through SCEIF and other social investment mechanisms might allow community enterprise to raise its sights and expand its vision and the scale both of its thinking and of its operation. If from the other side Government were to encourage community enterprise through legislative recognition and through various tax-breaks to ease private investment in community enterprise, then the stage would be set for the North Kensington Amenity Trusts and the Govan Workspaces to become the norm rather than the exceptions.

Chapter 11

Recognition before the law

"These associations would not subject the government to the same proportion of trouble and expense that an equal population would do in old society; on the contrary, they would relieve the government of the whole burden; and...would materially add to the political strength, power and resources of the country."

By its purpose and nature community enterprise is distinct from private business. This difference is reflected in the legal structures adopted by community enterprises. In Scotland, Community Business Scotland (CBS) has promoted a model constitution which was updated and revised early in 1992. This model has been accepted by the Inland Revenue as eligible for tax relief as a charity. The model is based on a membership company limited by guarantee (the Community Enterprise) and it will usually act as the holding company for a number of wholly-owned subsidiaries. It is also possible to jointly own subsidiaries with other companies or organisations. **Figure ix,** overleaf, illustrates the model structures.

In the Highlands and Islands a further model exists, the Community Co-operative, using the Industrial and Provident Societies Acts. This was first devised as part of the HIDB community co-operative package launched in 1977. In most key characteristics it is similar to the community company structure which has recently tended to supersede the co-operative structure for newly forming community enterprises in the north and west of Scotland.

In England and Wales there has been no comparable model constitution for community enterprises in general use, although the Industrial Common Ownership Movement (ICOM) launched a community business constitution in 1988 as part of its company formation service. It has been more difficult for English and Welsh community enterprises to obtain charitable status. Notwithstanding that, most community enterprises will

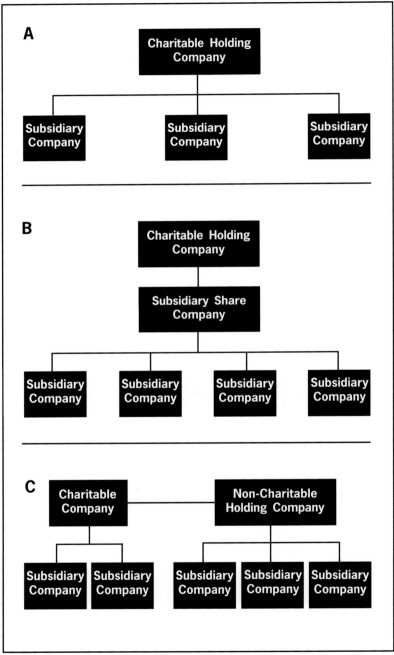

Figure ix Community Enterprise Model Legal Structures

have charitable status or will be linked in some way to an organisation which is accepted as a charity.

The Scottish model

The 1992 revised Scottish model constitution recognises five charitable objectives in the main objects clause:

1. the relief of poverty

2. the advancement of education

3. the promotion and/or provision of training in skills of all kinds, particularly such skills as will assist people in obtaining paid employment

4. the promotion, establishment and operation of other schemes of a charitable nature for the benefit of the community

5. the promotion of trade and industry for the benefit of the general public.

The 1992 revision also includes a provision to entrench the fundamental features of the constitution: those which are the essential difference between community enterprise and conventional private business. These features are:

a. the objects of the company

b. the inability of the company to distribute or transfer income or property to members

c. the holding of assets in trust for the community, such that any surplus assets on winding up may only go to community benefit

d. the voluntary principle of directors who are not paid for their work as directors

e. local community members always having a majority of the membership and a majority of places on the board of directors

f. the requirement to produce an annual report on social and community benefits: 'the social audit'.

The mechanism adopted to secure the entrenchment of these features is the appointment of a **special member** without whose consent changes to the relevant clauses and articles may not be made. The special member is likely to be a local authority, a community enterprise support organisation, a community enterprise federation (such as Community Business Scotland) or some other figure who would not allow any attempt to tamper, and so safeguard the essential characteristics of community enterprise. Such a provision is important because under company law otherwise a 75% vote of those members attending and actually voting at a special general meeting called for the purpose can make any fundamental change they wish. It would not be impossible therefore for the membership of a community enterprise to be run down to a small group and for that group quite legally to change the nature of the organisation from community enterprise to, say, a private company which could realise and distribute its assets for the private benefit of its members.[1]

The special member mechanism (not unlike the 'golden share') allows changes to be made when and if they are essential: for example, modifying the main objects clause in line with changing Inland Revenue rulings or in line with future changes to tax legislation.[2] An alternative mechanism would be to make any changes to the key characteristics subject to a unanimous vote of all registered members: a tough task in the event of a change being needed and there being a large membership; but no safeguard against the actions of a depleted membership. A variant to the unanimous vote is the 'responsible member' arrangement whereby a single member voting against the resolution is deemed to have sufficient votes to defeat the resolution. The disadvantage of this mechanism is that it leaves open the possibility of a bona fide change being blocked by a member who is being deliberately awkward. The special member provision introduces the notion of regulation, an issue to which we shall return later.

Problems of charitable status

Community enterprises have sought charitable status for the fiscal and other benefits which such status can confer. However even where a community enterprise is recognised as a charity there remains the problem that trading profits are generally considered to fall outwith the charitable exemption from tax. Indeed, more fundamentally, the provision of employment (for the able-bodied) is not itself considered to represent a charitable objective and therefore the charitable body must confine itself to a 'second-tier' role creating the conditions under which people in a state of poverty may find work. The trading activity of training is generally acceptable as a charitable activity, as is the running of a managed workspace which has a clear element of advice-giving and training as part of the management function.

For those community enterprises which have sought to operate within the charitable framework it has generally been necessary to adopt

complex and cumbersome structures, involving a charitable holding
company with non-charitable trading subsidiary or sister companies.
Surplus profits can be drawn from the trading companies in a tax-
efficient way by way of a deed of covenant or a qualifying donation
('gift aid') arrangement to the charity. However once drawn off into the
charity there are problems if the subsidiary later requires a cash injection
(and there is always a temptation to draw off apparently surplus funds in
order to minimise tax to the extent of leaving a subsidiary short of
liquidity). The role which the charitable holding company can
legitimately take (in terms of both charity and fiscal law) under such a
community enterprise structure and the extent to which it can give
financial assistance in relation to the establishment and/or ongoing
support of the trading enterprises is a continuing area of uncertainty.
Interpretation of the law can vary significantly around the country.

Charity law, originating in statutes of the seventeenth century, was not
designed for community enterprise activity. Yet community enterprises
are unequivocally about benefiting the community and their
constitutions embody the safeguards which are normally required in a
charity. The key difference is that community enterprises trade: it is by
doing business that they provide a benefit to their community, indeed
sometimes it is the very business itself which is the community benefit. It
is that which makes them different both from charities and from normal
business.

There is therefore a strong case to argue for this difference to be
recognised. Trying to be a charity is inappropriate and leads the
community enterprise down a road of complex structures and potential
administrative confusion. Yet because community enterprises are what
they are they should be able to qualify for some of the benefits which are
more usually associated with charities.

The case for legislative recognition

If there were legislative recognition of community enterprise which
offered a special fiscal status, the idea of community enterprise would
acquire a more generally accepted standing as well as avoiding the
inappropriate complexities of charity law.

A system of legislative recognition for community enterprise would
require to be based on a clear and enforceable understanding of what
constitutes a community enterprise. The key characteristics have been
stated earlier (chapter 3) and can be summarised as follows as regards
legislative recognition:

1. objectives

The primary purpose is to benefit the community by tackling economic, social and environmental problems; and to achieve this by trading and by other means.

2. use of profits

Community enterprises aim to make a profit from their trading, but the use of that profit is restricted to re-investment in the enterprise, to paying bonus schemes for workers in the enterprise and to funding schemes of community benefit (including the setting up of other enterprises). Profits are not distributed to members or directors and only a fixed and limited return is paid to any share-holders or to members who might lend capital.

3. assets

The assets of the enterprise are owned 'in trust' for the community and may not be realised in any way to make personal financial gain for members or for directors.

4. remuneration of directors and members

Directors and members may only receive payment insofar as they are workers or acting in an agreed key executive capacity; simply acting as a director is no entitlement to remuneration or to a share of profits.

5. accountability

The community enterprise structure should ensure that the members of the community which the enterprise has been set up to benefit have a major role in influencing and controlling the affairs of the enterprise.

Regulation

A system of legislative recognition will require some form of national register and regulation to ensure that only genuine community enterprises are recognised. Regulation would include:

1. **approval of community enterprise constitutions** to ensure that in each case they adequately enshrine the key characteristics noted above.

2. a test of **localness** to ensure that the area of benefit was such that people could reasonably identify with it.

3. the requirement that each recognised community enterprise submitted, in addition to its audited accounts, an annual **community benefit report** detailing how it had fulfilled the terms of its main objects during the previous year.

It would not be necessary to create a new form of corporate structure for community enterprises as existing company legislation and the industrial and provident societies acts can adequately provide for incorporation with limited liability. A regulatory body for community enterprises (see below) should however approve a small number of model constitutions, such as the Community Business Scotland model, so that there is an easily adopted and nationally accepted constitutional form. However as model constitutions are often 'tailored' to suit local circumstances or wishes and this flexibility is an important advantage, it will be necessary for the regulatory body to examine each adopted constitution for approval prior to inclusion on the national register. The regulatory body might routinely act as the 'special member' having to approve any constitutional amendments.

The test of localness would need to strike a balance between an area small enough for people to identify with but big enough to be a viable area of operation. As we saw in an earlier chapter, size will vary according to local circumstances and function but the regulatory body will require to be persuaded in each case by evidence put forward by the promoters of the community enterprise of the appropriateness of the area proposed. Such a process is not unlike the present role of the Registrar of Friendly Societies[3] having to satisfy himself that the proposed 'common bond' area for a credit union is sufficiently big and sufficiently 'common'. The task of agreeing on the area of benefit and consulting the various stake-holders would in itself be a valuable exercise for the partners in a community enterprise initiative.

Reporting on community benefit must be the quid pro quo of community enterprises enjoying benefits from special legislative recognition. The 1992 revision of the CBS model constitution includes provision for the directors of the company to "arrange for an objective assessment to be made on an annual basis of the social and community benefits achieved by the company; the social audit, in addition to examining the effectiveness of the company in relation to pursuit of its objects, shall address matters bearing upon the welfare of employees".[4]

The Regulatory Body could be either part of an existing statutory organisation, or a self-regulatory authority created by the community enterprise movement or some form of new National Community Enterprise Agency. The preferred option would be the last; a small UK national agency which operated under the control of a joint board representing community enterprises, government and private finance and industry, perhaps with an independent chair drawn from a major trust or foundation with an interest in the community economy or drawn from an academic institution. The creation of a new body would of itself further accord recognition to community enterprise as an approved means of achieving local development.

An important task of the Regulatory Body will be to ensure that the legislative provisions for community enterprises are not abused by bodies masquerading as having community benefit objectives. This will require tight monitoring of annual reports - both financial and community benefit - with particular regard to any attempts by the unscrupulous to transfer assets to directors or members by such means as inflated salaries or management fees. One means of ensuring adequate monitoring safeguards could be to develop a register of approved auditors for community enterprises. The register would include both those who conduct the annual financial audit and those approved as competent to do the community benefit audit (see chapter 12).

It will also be necessary to ensure by monitoring that registered community enterprises are not unfairly competing against other small local firms. In part this fear of unfair competition is answered by the very nature of community enterprises tending to undertake work not done by the private sector. But operating rules will require to be framed and monitored not unlike those guidelines drawn up by the Scottish Office for use of urban programme grant to support community businesses. These made clear that grant-aid shall not "subsidise unrealistically high (wage) payments...nor artificially low prices".[5]

Positive discrimination

Legislative recognition for community enterprise could most easily be achieved through the means of an appropriate clause in a future Finance Act in the same way as the 1982 Finance Act (consolidated in the Income and Corporation Taxes Act 1988) introduced the concept of the Local Enterprise Agency (LEA) and provided that a contribution to an approved LEA is deducted when computing trading profits for tax purposes.

The key benefits which might thereafter be sought for approved community enterprises are:

1. exemption from corporation tax

2. the ability to receive covenants and donations in the same way as a charity

3. 100% rates relief

4. permission for public authorities to transfer property and other assets to community enterprises at less than the District Valuer or open market valuations

5. permission for public authorities to operate a discretion of up to 5% in favour of community enterprises when awarding local contracts.

It has been accepted policy in the United States for some time for public agency procurement sections to discriminate in favour of minority businesses (ie black or hispanic) when awarding contracts, usually to a guaranteed minimum percentage value of all contracts awarded. Similarly Glasgow District used to operate a five per cent discretion in favour of local small firms. A similar arrangement operated in favour of community enterprises would go some way to ensuring that public sector procurement of goods and services was able to directly contribute to job creation in local communities of high unemployment. A modification in the terms of the compulsory competitive tendering legislation would be required to permit such a policy to be applied to most public sector contracting.

In addition to these specific benefits it is considered that legislative recognition would make it easier for both the public and the private sectors to support and work with community enterprises. Recognition would bring with it an official sanction and the implication that supporting the community enterprise model was considered to be an appropriate mechanism for local development initiatives. It would permit the public sector to discriminate in favour of such organisations, knowing that public funds were only being used for community gain and not for personal profit.

For similar reasons it would make it more comfortable for private sector organisations to provide a range of support, and would extricate community enterprises from the dilemma in which they sometimes find themselves when seeking assistance from the private sector: too commercial to be helped by the community support programmes which are for 'charitable' work, yet not commercial enough for support from the business or investment sections.

Links between co-operative and community enterprise

The Industrial Common Ownership Act of 1976 was special legislation (a private member's bill) to define workers' co-operatives and to establish a registration system for those seeking financial

assistance from a fund established under the Act. While a specific Act of
Parliament is not considered necessary at this stage in the case of
community enterprise the ICO Act does represent a useful precedent
of both definition and a registration system.

At its first Annual Forum meeting in 1992 the UK Co-operative
Council[6] approved a six point plan calling for government to instigate
a wide-ranging review of public policy towards co-operatives. Their
proposals include a Co-operative Societies Act, the establishment of a
Co-operative Commission, positive fiscal discrimination in favour of
co-operatives and financial support for development work and training
within the co-operative sector. These proposals are not significantly
different from ideas being advocated within the community enterprise
sector and by the present writer. Indeed in legislative terms many
organisations which can be considered as community enterprises are
registered as co-operative societies (credit unions, community-based
housing associations and co-operatives, some community co-
operatives in the Highlands and Islands). Conversely a majority of
worker co-operatives are now registered as companies limited by
guarantee.

The Community Business Scotland Legal Structures Working Party has
advocated the relevance for a community enterprise to sponsor the
formation of local worker co-operatives as the appropriate business
structure for some activities (**figure iii** and the discussion in chapter 4).
A working model for a workers co-operative linked to a community
business has been developed whereby the co-operative operates within
the community enterprise framework but as an operationally
independent business fully under the control of its workforce. The
model permits the community enterprise to control, by way of a
'special member', the distribution of assets, changes in the co-
operative's constitution and any 'unusual' pay increase proposals.
Where a profit share is to be paid to the working members of the co-
operative the amount must be matched by an equal payment to the
charitable community enterprise.[7] In Middlesbrough a successful
workers co-operative in the building industry operates as part of the East
Middlesbrough Community Venture group.

For the long-term any thorough-going review of public policy with a
view to new legislation should encompass both community and co-
operative enterprise which together make up what is increasingly
referred to as the 'Social Economy'. There is more common ground
than difference and indeed, as recounted earlier, one historical root of

community enterprise was the pioneering collective action of the Toad Lane co-operators in 1844. Their counterparts are to be found in most poor and disadvantaged communities today, running credit unions, setting up a food co-operative, planning a community enterprise.

The key point of distinction which lies between the community enterprise sector and part of the co-operative sector is to do with the deployment of profit and the use of assets: whether the co-operative exists primarily to deliver personal financial gain exclusively to its members or whether it has wider ideals of benefit.

The nub of the argument in favour of community enterprise being accorded a special status through legislative recognition and consequently receiving certain fiscal benefits and other preferential treatment, is that they exist to benefit the community and not to offer personal financial gain to directors or members, beyond reasonable reward for work done.

Chapter 12

Auditing the community benefit

"But the practice of everything new, however trifling, requires time and experience to perfect it. It cannot be expected that arrangements which comprehend the whole business of life, and reduce to practice the entire science of political economy, can at once be combined and executed in the best manner. Many errors will be at first committed; and, as in every other attempt by human means to unite a great variety of parts to produce one grand result, many partial failures may be anticipated."

Community Enterprise is about development which tackles economic, social and environmental problems and delivers a benefit to the community. This is what Hazel Henderson has called "sustainable, equitable development",[1] sensitive to the needs of the human race and to the needs of the resource system called the planet earth on which we live. It is what others call people-centred development in contrast to development which is centred on profit maximisation and wealth creation for the few.

Auditing is about verifying what has been done and providing an accurate statement of profit and loss and of net worth. Social auditing has been used as the term to mean systems of verifying and measuring the non-commercial outcomes of business (and indeed other) activity. Sometimes the phrase 'social accounting' has been used.[2] To some degree 'social' is a limiting word because it implies a focus only on social issues such as welfare and recreation. We shall therefore use the rather more cumbersome phrase Community Benefit Audit in order to focus attention on the need to develop ways of measuring the various outcomes of community enterprise in terms of their beneficial (or not) impact on the community and on the planet and its people.

Defining benefit

That implies making judgements about what is beneficial and what is not: and indeed the idea that society can and should make certain choices about what is good and what is not good for the planet and its people does lie at the heart of the debate. Current measurement of development tends to be simply in terms of growth: growth as measured by GNP. If there is growth, there is benefit. That crudely measures that which can be counted, money, per capita income. There is no distinction between benefits or dis-benefits to society: people or the environment. Thus cleaning up after pollution spillages, coping with major car accidents, cutting down rain forests, advertising to encourage people to smoke, waging war and producing arms: all add to economic growth. But growth of what? and to what end? Growth is a blunt instrument which can damage as much, sometimes more, than it benefits.

Hazel Henderson has proposed the idea of a "sin tax" to be placed on products or activities which are known to have harmful effects on people or the planet. Dr Peter Draper has suggested a similar scheme so that manufacturers might bear the social cost of, for example, increased tooth decay from sugar-coated cereals.[3] This 'polluter pays' principle has gained some credence and is now being applied in some environmental contexts where companies are expected to include the cost of land re-instatement and reparation in any development proposal. The proposed EC carbon tax is a good example.

Traditional counting of economic activity only counts that which is 'monetised', thus entirely overlooking the unmonetised part of the economy: household work and family care, DIY and vegetable growing, neighbourly assistance and volunteering, the informal 'black' economy. In terms of the Third World it ignores most subsistence agriculture such that "nearly half the world's population and over half the inhabitants of the Third World are statistically invisible in economic terms".[4] Traditional counting also ignores the depletion of the world's natural resources and the cost to the planet in terms of toxic wastes, despoliation of the atmosphere and the waterways and the future, largely hidden costs, of coping with that pollution.

Different ways of measuring the outcome of development are required which take the stance of assessing benefit to people and to the planet. Current business financial auditing and traditional GNP and growth measures entirely miss this.[5]

Defining profit

Community Benefit Audits, when applied to community enterprises, are based on the assumption that those enterprises have, through their operation, a community impact which will be beneficial. The Community Benefit Audit will measure that impact and establish a framework within which the true profit, in its widest sense, of the community enterprise can be assessed.

A business with a healthy profitable bottom line in its financial report could be causing a range of dis-benefits, the costs of which are unwittingly absorbed by customers or employees, or are met by local or central government or are just ignored as uncountable. Conversely a community enterprise which provides a demonstrable benefit to local people in its community may show a loss at the bottom line. Conventional wisdom dictates that the community enterprise should close down as a failed business while the 'profitable' business will be hailed as a success of entrepreneurship.

This should not be taken to imply that a community enterprise will ipso facto show a net community benefit; indeed one of the important outcomes of introducing a system of community benefit auditing is to make it possible to assess whether community enterprises do produce a worthwhile community profit and therefore justify public investment in them.

Most community benefit audit work of the past has been of the 'negative' type: that is assessing the dis-benefits which will occur if a company were to take a particular course of action. Thus studies will be carried out on the impact the closure of a plant may have on the locality. Such studies may be used to try and prevent closure, or to ensure that government or the company in question takes remedial action to soften the worst potential effects of redundancy, unemployment and other related problems. Experience of the last 20 years has shown that closures can rarely be averted; they may be delayed for political reasons but seldom in order to embark on a serious development process ahead of the crisis so as to minimise social dislocation.[6] Mostly new initiatives come after closure has happened and are too little, too late. The social costs of closures are mainly borne by society at large through public sector expenditure and do not count against the profitability of the withdrawing company or industry.

Another type of negative impact audit will assess the probable impact if a particular project were to be carried through. These have generally had

an environmental focus and it is in this area that there has been good
publicity and some success. Recent notable examples have included the
high speed rail route in Kent and the Hinkley Point power station inquiry.
The growing concern about environmental issues has had a noticeable
impact on what society now demands by way of landscape reparation
and pollution controls. For example, CFCs are to be phased out (albeit
not fast enough), the supermarkets are full of 'environmentally friendly'
products, major companies take television time to advertise how well
they repair the landscape after major disruptive developments. It is
however noticeable how more alive our public concern seems to be for
the impact of development and industry on the environment than on the
people who used to provide the labour but are now no longer wanted.

A practical audit model for community enterprise

Discussion about developing a community benefit audit methodology
and process has been long-standing but little practical progress has been
achieved. The 'social audit model' reproduced as **figure x** first appeared
in the 1986/87 annual report of Strathclyde Community Business and
later in issue no 29 of the *CB News* (May/June 1989).

There are three main problems: first, deciding what data should be
gathered and how; second, working out ways in which the value of
unmonetised benefits can be assessed and presented; and third, the actual
cost of such an exercise.

Some practical work has been done in Scotland to produce a method for
experimentation. A first principle or parameter adopted was that the
community benefit audit should not on average cost, on an annual basis,
more than the conventional financial audit any company is obliged by
law to complete. Implicit was the notion that there should be an annual
community benefit audit to appear alongside the financial audit to set the
framework within which the financial performance can be re-assessed.
This requirement for an annual community benefit audit has been
included in the revised version of the CBS model community business
constitution (see page 104).

A second principle was that just as an enterprise must keep adequate
financial records, so it should also keep adequate community benefit
records so that there is information to verify and on which to base an
audit report at the end of the year.

The third principle was that an external community benefit auditor
should be engaged to produce the annual report.

THE SOCIAL AUDIT CHECK LIST

OBJECTIVE	QUESTIONS	COST TO THE COMMUNITY BUSINESS	VALUE TO SOCIETY
1. TO CREATE JOBS FOR LOCAL PEOPLE	How many? For whom? Were the workers previously unemployed? or disadvantaged in some other way (eg disabled)? Where do the workers live? Are the jobs full-time or part-time?	What training is provided? What are the implications for productivity in employing workers who were previously unemployed, especially long-term unemployed? How long does it take people to get used to working again?	What savings are there in welfare benefits no longer paid? How much tax and NI is paid by those workers? How much additional money is circulating in the local economy from the payment of wages?
2. TO PROVIDE LOCAL SERVICES	What commercial services are provided locally? (eg workspace, local security patrol, laundrette, enterprise training). How effective are they? What social services are provided or managed by the Community business? (eg thrift shop, minibus, community workshop). Would these services exist without the Community Business?	Does the Community Business need to subsidise any of these services? How much management time is devoted to social service provision?	How much money is spent in the local community that otherwise would have been spent elsewhere? What rents and rates does the local authority get from buildings previously unused. What "spin-off" community benefits are there? What local improvements can be identified?
3. TO BE GOOD EMPLOYERS	Are wages and conditions good? What is the level of job satisfaction? What training opportunities are provided? Have those on training programmes moved on to full-time jobs? Do workers move on to better job opportunities? What mechanisms are there for worker participation, and do they work?	What is the cost of the training provision in terms of staff time and any fees paid? Does worker participation make for more efficiency? Is it a cost to the company?	How do levels of wages, conditions, job satisfaction and job creation compare with other local employers?
4. TO SET UP A COMMUNITY OWNED AND CONTROLLED ENTERPRISE	How many members or shareholders are there? What information is provided for them? Are they interested and involved? How are new people encouraged to become involved? How many directors are there? How active are they? What training is provided for them and for members? In what ways is the business accountable through its members to the community?	How much staff time is taken-up in these "non-commercial" aspects? How much does it cost to make Community Business democracy work?	Do members/directors get involved in other aspects of community life? Do they learn skills which are useful in other projects? Do individuals gain in experience and confidence?
5. TO BENEFIT THE COMMUNITY	What community benefit projects/activities are undertaken? (eg Community Programme schemes). What community benefit services are offered? (eg use of premises and equipment, of secretarial services, of transport). What other benefits have taken place? (eg buildings improved, act as information centre). What have been the "hidden" benefits? (eg less vandalism, improved morale, sense of purpose, health, environment). Do other groups visit to find out about Community Business?	What does it cost the CB to provide these direct community benefits in terms of staff time and money? How commercially disruptive is it?	How many short-term jobs and training opportunities have been provided? How many have moved on to full-time jobs? What physical improvements have occurred? Are the "hidden" benefits noticeable?
6. TO USE PROFITS FOR COMMUNITY BENEFIT	Are there profits? If so, how are they used? - reinvested in the business's enterprises? - invested in new enterprises? - grants for local groups and activities?	How much is spent non-commercially? (eg on football strips, Christmas parties or Gala days)	What new projects have been created because of the Community Business's investment?
7. TO ACT AS A FOCUS FOR LOCAL ECONOMIC AND COMMUNITY DEVELOPMENT	Is the Community Business active in local community affairs? What has it done, how effectively and with what results? Have any new economic or community development activities been promoted? Is the Community Business a channel for new investment into the area?	How much time and other resources are devoted to community development activities rather than to running the business?	How much new money has come into the community through the activities of the Community Business? Is the Community Business recognised and contracted by the local authority and other public bodies?

Figure x The Social Audit Check List

The process which has been devised can be equally applicable to any enterprise or organisation which professes to have in some way 'community benefit objectives'. The process has been introduced to a group of five worker co-operatives in Nottinghamshire.[7]

The process comprises four stages:

1. Defining the community benefit objectives

An enterprise must clearly define just what its community benefit objectives are. Indeed for a community enterprise these are the key objectives which the enterprise's trading activities are designed to serve or to fulfil.

The planning exercise should concentrate on realistic objectives and on getting those involved to recognise the community benefit of some of the activities which they just take for granted. Usually objectives will be ranked in order of priority and it may be that they will divide into 'primary' and 'secondary' objectives.

2. Agreeing the action strategies for achieving community benefit

The enterprise requires to clarify and agree what it is doing/intends to do in order to achieve its stated community benefit objectives. This exercise equally must concentrate on realistic and practical intentions to avoid the enterprise setting itself impossible targets.

3. Setting up the community benefit book-keeping system

A record-keeping system requires to be set up which permits the enterprise to record regularly and systematically the information which it is agreed is needed to establish whether it does produce the community benefit it has aimed to give and to measure the effectiveness of that benefit. The recording system must be simple, easy to keep and be cost - and time - effective.

The community benefit book-keeping should also record the cost to the enterprise of delivering its community benefit. In some cases it will be minimal or the benefit will be an integral part of carrying out straightforward commercial work. In other cases the cost can be substantial, but hidden, especially when employee time is involved. Time spent on providing community benefit may be time not spent on productive working and thus contribute to financial unprofitability.

The enterprise itself has the primary responsibility for keeping the books. Some information may require to be entered daily, other weekly or less frequently. Often the information required for the community benefit audit will be little different from the information that is already (or should be) held: employee records, training records, time management information, spending on community benefit projects. Recording systems will need to be customised to the circumstances of each enterprise. Always they must be simple and those responsible for keeping the books must understand the relevance of doing so.

4. The annual community benefit audit

During the course of the year the enterprise should use its community benefit records to produce ongoing management reports for consideration by employees and directors. Keeping on top of what is being achieved (or not) and how much it costs is as important a part of community enterprise management as is keeping close control over the commercial activities.

Each year the external community benefit auditor will produce a report based on:

a. verifying and checking the information contained in the community benefit records

b. a first impact survey conducted with a small sample of the main community beneficiaries (in some cases there will be several groups of beneficiaries according to the range of activities in which the enterprise is involved)

c. a second impact survey conducted with a small reference group considered to be representative of the wider community.

The audit report should:

i. describe and quantify the exact nature of the community benefit achieved and identify failures to achieve objectives

ii. explain the cost to the enterprise of achieving the benefit

iii. where possible, calculate the value of the community benefit in terms of cost savings to the public purse

iv. where not possible, describe and assess from a.- c. above and especially from the second impact survey the nature and perceived value of the community benefit which cannot be converted into money terms

v. make recommendations about changes to the community benefit objectives, the strategies to achieve them and the record-keeping system.

Stages one to three above assume that the community enterprise is already in existence and that it is necessary to introduce a community benefit auditing system from scratch. In such circumstances the external auditor should be involved to assist with the objective setting, clarifying the strategies and agreeing a sensible record-keeping system.

Rigorous planning

In an ideal situation however all this planning will have taken place at the outset with a community benefit plan forming part of the original business plan for the enterprise. Indeed those agencies which support community enterprises should be making investment decisions on the basis not only of the commercial business plan but also on the basis of the community benefit plan. In a situation of scarce resources where commercial prospects appear similar, it will be the community enterprise that promises the greater community benefit which should receive the investment. Further, investing agencies need to know exactly what it is that the community enterprise intends to do. Too often there is undue focus on the commercial business plan, and in some circumstances the community benefit objectives are played down or even hidden for fear of detracting from the acceptability of the business plan.

The community enterprise will use the community benefit audit report to evaluate its community benefit performance and to make appropriate adjustments. There is a close convergence of the community benefit and the commercial because the audit allows the enterprise to see the relationship between commercial performance and community benefit. At the end of the day community benefit which jeopardises the survival of the enterprise is the ultimate dis-benefit.

All enterprises must plan and re-plan in the face of external forces. An enterprise which professes both commercial and community benefit objectives must plan both aspects in an integrated fashion. Too often the commercial business is planned and the community benefit left to happen informally: and that can result either in community benefit being ignored or, in total contrast, stealthily taking over. Lay directors may take more interest in planning the community benefit side and leave the commercial to the managers and then not understand what is happening, or find themselves in conflict with management. In other situations there is no planning on either front. The community benefit audit process is quite simply about ensuring that a community enterprise has an effective planning and monitoring process which connects community benefit aspirations to the commercial side of the enterprise. Keeping a proper balance between these two is the essential sustainable balance which community enterprises must strive to attain.

Figure xi illustrates how business planning and community benefit planning should follow a similar, and parallel course. The planning for each part of the enterprise should be equally rigorous and at all stages cross-referenced to ensure that the one is not in any way adversely affecting the other.

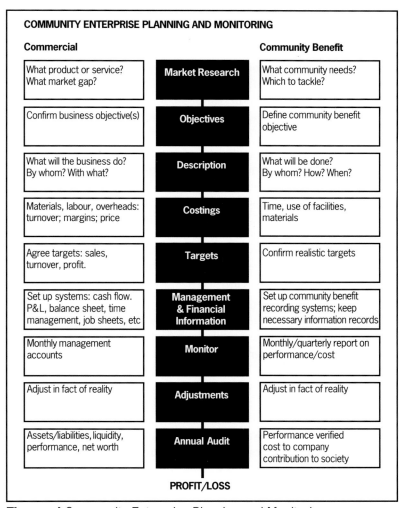

COMMUNITY ENTERPRISE PLANNING AND MONITORING

Commercial		Community Benefit
What product or service? What market gap?	**Market Research**	What community needs? Which to tackle?
Confirm business objective(s)	**Objectives**	Define community benefit objective
What will the business do? By whom? With what?	**Description**	What will be done? By whom? How? When?
Materials, labour, overheads: turnover; margins; price	**Costings**	Time, use of facilities, materials
Agree targets: sales, turnover, profit.	**Targets**	Confirm realistic targets
Set up systems: cash flow. P&L, balance sheet, time management, job sheets, etc	**Management & Financial Information**	Set up community benefit recording systems; keep necessary information records
Monthly management accounts	**Monitor**	Monthly/quarterly report on performance/cost
Adjust in fact of reality	**Adjustments**	Adjust in fact of reality
Assets/liabilities, liquidity, performance, net worth	**Annual Audit**	Performance verified cost to company contribution to society

PROFIT/LOSS

Figure xi Community Enterprise Planning and Monitoring

123

Reporting to the public

The community benefit audit can also be used by the enterprise to demonstrate to a wider audience just what the enterprise does contribute to society and taken together with the financial audit it will offer a rounded report on the performance of the enterprise. That report could form the basis of contracts between the public sector and the enterprise to provide certain clear community benefits. Indeed if community enterprises are to have some form of special status which reflects the unique contribution they can make to local development, then there should be an absolute requirement on them not only to report on community benefit performance but also to analyse and measure it. Indeed it should be a condition of public sector investment in, and positive discrimination in favour of, community enterprise that community benefit plans form part of the initial business plan and that community benefit audits are carried out annually by accredited auditors.

From 1993 Traidcraft will undertake a formal social audit by appointing independent assessors to look at company performance in non-financial areas including producer impact, environmental impact and personnel policies. This social audit scheme has been developed by the New Economics Foundation.[8] It would also be an interesting comparison to apply the process to some straightforward small and medium-sized private businesses which, where locally rooted as part of the local community, might compare quite favourably in terms of community benefit to some community enterprises.

During the Wilson government of the middle 1970s there was an attempt by Tony Benn, when at the Department of Trade, to link financial support for industry with agreed community benefits through some form of planning agreement. Although this was never officially implemented a number of local authorities at the time experimented with informal agreements with companies in their areas. The concept has recently been re-emerging. Companies tendering for contracts in the east European states are finding that the governments of those 'emerging democracies' want to know not just the tender price but also what the company proposes to offer with regard to other economic reconstruction. It has become almost a matter of routine now for companies to report voluntarily on their environmental impacts, keeping ahead of legislative requirements about the disclosure of such information.

In a contract culture it is not unreasonable for public investment in any enterprise to demand particular returns for society. Those returns should be quite specific and measurable, and they should have regard to the impact of any proposed investment on both people and the planet. By adopting a voluntary system of rigorous community benefit auditing the community enterprise movement would be setting a standard.

It is reported that the DOE is now talking of the legitimacy of 'soft' as well as 'hard' outcomes from public (and private) investment in urban regeneration. That seems to accept the principle that not all outcomes can be measured in a simple £p way. But equally 'soft' outcomes must be the subject of effective planning and target-setting so that performance can be measured. The criteria for measurement will be different. Once the principle of 'soft' outcomes is accepted, the way is open for government and local government to contract with community enterprises to deliver those soft outcomes and be paid for doing so.

Early in 1992 the Per Cent Club, a BITC off-shoot of companies which promise to contribute 0.5% of their profits to the community, published a booklet advising its members of the value both of reporting their community activities in detail and quantifying the cost/ value of those activities where this is possible. Although a major stimulus to these suggestions is to do with corporate image and public relations, the notion of reporting and quantifying is established. Writing in *The Guardian* at the time Roger Cowe pointed to the next step:

"Measuring outputs, as the economists would put it, is not as easy as measuring costs. But the Per Cent Club might consider telling its members to try, so readers of their community reports might learn about the effectiveness of companies' efforts, not just the extent of those efforts. Then, of course, companies' claims will have to be verified independently, and BITC will have to re-invent social auditing." Just so.

Chapter 13

Beyond 2000: community enterprise for the twenty-first century

"The past ages of the world present the history of human irrationality only, and that we are but now advancing towards the dawn of reason, and to the period when the mind of man shall be born again."

"There is another way": the Coin Street slogan emphasises that community enterprise is about local development based on a set of values quite different from the private sector and also quite different from the public sector in action. It is about development which is people-centred and which is sustainable: that is beneficial to people and to the planet. These objectives override the traditional business objectives of personal wealth creation and return on investment. Community enterprise does not distinguish between economic and social, the two are completely entwined; indeed it is the belief that there can be economic 'development' without regard to social implications that has led and continues to lead to so many world problems. Because community enterprise is about community-led development it empowers local people to exert some control over their local destiny.

World-wide there are organisations and individuals adopting the same values and the same holistic approach.[1] Community enterprise in Britain is a part of a much broader movement, a movement which as its ultimate goal has the objective of changing the value base of the world's political and economic systems; to make the economy work for people, to ensure that all 'development' is in the interests of the majority of mankind and its planet and not just for the benefit of a few.

These are grand sounding goals, but the world does face a uniquely serious set of problems which could irrevocably ruin the life chances on this planet for future generations. We cannot stand idly by hoping that it will not happen, that something will 'turn up'. Those involved in community enterprise are doing something practical to change their own situation. But that something practical is rooted in a wider vision of what might be for all mankind: think global, act local.

In Britain it is important that community enterprise holds to its ideals and values. All around there is pressure to become 'just like any other business'. The fact is that community enterprise is not like any other business and, if it is true to itself, should never want to be. There is a regrettable tendency to hide the differences and emphasise the sameness. The opposite should be the policy for it is in the difference that lies its strength, its attraction and, eventually, its moral force.

Practically, however, there is a niche in the economy for community enterprise: as the 'lead' business structure in the community economy, responsible for a range of business and project activities which we have seen are appropriately controlled and managed at local community level. For such activities the notions of service and quality should be more important than profit. This could be an important outcome from applying the principle of subsidiarity to domestic affairs: giving local communities real responsibility for local services and aspects of local development. Community enterprises should be seen as the appropriate mechanism or structure combining, as they do, business-like operation within a non-profit distributing framework, commercial effectiveness applied to community benefit.

It will not be possible to prescribe 'local' and 'community' as a set size geographically or as regards population, but there must be some test of 'localness' to ensure that there is some sense of identity with the area being proposed. Nor should we be too anxious about overlap and duplication: after all real life is a rich pattern of overlapping interests and activities and community enterprise must be allowed to reflect that pattern at the local level (**figure iv**).

The community economy comes at the interface of the formal and the informal economies, at the place where unpaid and paid meet. The community enterprise is a creature of the community economy. It should be able to support and encourage all and any activities which impact on the local economy. That can include as we have seen (**figure v**) voluntary enterprises as well as commercially viable community businesses.

Indeed as unemployment climbs even higher with no realistic expectation of a return to 'full employment' (after all some communities have been waiting for more than a generation for that to come about), it is more important than ever to blur the distinction between paid and unpaid. It is equally as relevant - certainly in terms of numbers affected - for local development to concentrate on enterprises or projects which reduce the cost of living (voluntary run launderettes or cafes, credit unions for example) as it is to create businesses which provide a number of full-time jobs. Community enterprise should legitimately be encouraging and be involved in a wide range of enterprising initiatives within the community economy which, taken together, will assist the greatest number of people achieve a reasonable livelihood.

The adoption of a basic citizen income scheme would do much to release the energy which exists within the community economy but which is now constrained by the available to work and casual employment rules of the benefit system.[2] Is it too much to hope that the enterprise rehearsal scheme within ET[3] and the self-employment credit scheme piloted in Cleveland[4] might be harbingers of things to come?

The location of much community enterprise at the edge of the informal economy and in communities on the margins of society can give rise to another problem. Many of the people connected to community enterprises operate partly in and partly out of the illegitimate informal economy: that is how people survive in areas of poverty and high unemployment. Their alternative value standards do not always sit comfortably with the 'squeaky clean' standards of legitimacy required by projects in receipt of public funds. That can create conflict and moral dilemmas for those involved both in management and in support agencies.

Community enterprises are distinctive both by what they do and how they are set up. Their structures for the most part define the value base and in particular emphasise the creation and holding of assets for community benefit and the non-distribution of profits to members and/ or directors. In French they are neatly described as being 'sans but lucratif': they exist to achieve community benefit. As such they are akin to charities, but on the whole they may not be charities because their main means of achieving their objectives is by trading, and trading is not deemed to be a charitable activity. Charity law, although used by community enterprises, is inappropriate.

What would be appropriate would be for society, through the government, to recognise the distinctiveness, the value and the desirability of the community enterprise method and model, and to grant it legislative recognition. Along with such a move should come some form of national registration or accreditation and a national Community Enterprise Agency to act as the regulatory body. Such recognition would open the way to fiscal and other public policy discrimination in favour of community enterprises on the grounds that society would prefer certain functions within the community economy to be done by community enterprises which are driven by notions of community betterment rather than private profit.

A national body would have the tasks of monitoring legal structures and monitoring the performance of community enterprises both financially and as regards the achievement of their community benefit plans. This will require agreeing new ways of measuring community benefit or profit and accepting the close inter-relationship between economic activity and social outcomes. A key ingredient in any measuring system will be setting and agreeing clear objectives so that performance can be assessed, and installing simple but effective methods for recording information. It is suggested that a register of approved 'community benefit auditors' be maintained by the national body.

Implicit in the suggestion that community benefit is a desired and assessable outcome from community enterprise is the acceptance first, that it may not be possible to measure the outcome in figures, especially £p and second, that there will be certain outcomes which community enterprises will provide which must be paid for otherwise than from their commercial trading activities. However the way to fund these desired outcomes is not through subsidy but through contracts. Society, whether through government, local government, quango, trust or private organisation, should contract with community enterprises to do certain things which are over and above what can sensibly be achieved within the framework of commercially priced contracts. Thus a hairdressing enterprise might be contracted to cut x heads of hair in pensioners' homes; a landscaping enterprise might be contracted to recruit x number of the local long-term unemployed each year and 'throughput' them over the year into vocational training or the wider labour market. A 'core community enterprise' will be contracted to do development work in the community economy.

The concept of the core community enterprise should be emphasised (see chapters 3 and 4 and **figures iii, iv and v**). Essentially it recognises that within the community economy there is development work to be done, helping establish the various elements of community enterprise which go to make up a thriving community economy. In the early 1980s this was neatly called 'animation'.

That work should be recognised as part of the job of a community enterprise designated as 'core community enterprise' in an agreed area and it must also be recognised that such work will not usually be fundable from the trading and revenue earned by the various business and project activities. This is a problematic funding gap: if it is unmet either the core community enterprise will fold up or, equally damaging as regards the development of the community, the development work will be dropped and the community enterprise become indistinguishable from any other small business. The potential for growth across the broad spectrum of community economic activity would be lost. What is required is recognition that the development work of a community enterprise is an essential and valuable part of its overall work and that it requires to be funded. Is it too much to expect TECs or LECs to contract with core community enterprises in their area to undertake this essential community development?

Community enterprises tend to have been set up in areas of poverty and industrial decline for the very good reason that the need is there and, in the face of adversity, people experience a common bond and a willingness to work together to do something. The concepts behind community enterprise should not however just be seen as relevant to poor or marginal communities: that would be to diminish both the idea and the ideals. However as with all programmes of social change it is not surprising that the starting point is where the problems are perceived and felt to be the greatest.

Community enterprises have been much studied over the years but they have been ill-researched in the sense of rigorous investigation like that commissioned by the Scottish office in 1987.[5] Too many reports about community enterprise have been based on anecdotal case-study and interviews with the same group of people, all interpreted by consultants with their own personal notions. If community enterprise is to be a serious part of the future way of running an important part of our economy, then there is an urgent need for effective research from which hard lessons can be drawn. The following topics are a starting list:

● an examination of community enterprises which have failed: what did they do? why did they fail? A preliminary exploration of this in Strathclyde in 1990 showed up a large number of human problems but also indicated that community enterprises were failing commercially in part because they were attempting to employ too many unemployed local people too fast.

- what makes a successful community enterprise manager?

- are community enterprises good employers?

- who do community enterprises employ and what happens to them when they leave that employment? The Scottish research[6] suggested that community enterprises are very effective at getting local people into work.

- just what community enterprises are there in the country? The map for England and Wales is very inadequately drawn, with particular regard to what was earlier called the 'business or trading sub-sector'.

Taking all the forms of community enterprise together: development trusts, community companies and co-operatives of all types, credit unions, community-based housing associations and co-operatives, to say nothing of the other trusts and voluntary organisations that are probably community enterprises but don't know it, there is a vast range of activity involving a very large number of people and turning over significant sums. Taken together that is a major force in local development.

Unfortunately it is not on the whole taken together. Indeed one of the big issues facing the whole community enterprise sector is how it can pull together to realise the clout it undoubtedly could - should - have. At the BITC Investing in Community Enterprise conference held early in 1992 a proposal was made to create some form of 'standing conference' of all types of community enterprise organisation, to begin at the very least a process of dialogue. Such a move would be a useful, if small, step forward. However we saw earlier that similar dialogue is relevant and necessary with the co-operative sector if a full alliance is to be created within that part of the economy which is based on the values described.

Creating an alliance is essential if the sector can speak with the powerful voice it ought to be able to employ. Speaking with such a voice will also make it harder for politicians to ignore it, and it is important that the community enterprise idea be espoused by a serious political party as part of the desired way forward.

The strength and success of the biggest community enterprises in Britain lies to a large degree in their acquisition of assets, usually property. This absolute ownership gives not only a good balance sheet item, it also gives credibility and a strong sense of self-esteem. If as a society we can become serious about subsidiarity then it is entirely appropriate for assets to be translated to community ownership and control. That is a process of empowering and it is also about giving and accepting responsibility.

Community enterprise operating at the local level in partnership and co-operation with other 'stake-holders' and in alliance with other community enterprises locally, nationally and internationally: that is a powerful idea - truly another way of doing things.

References

Introduction

1. The source of this and all subsequent chapter heading quotes (and that at the head of Appendix i) is: *A New View of Society and Other Writings*, Robert Owen, Penguin edition, 1991.

Chapter 1

1. *Community Trading Organisations: a review of community enterprise characteristics and practices*, Currie, McCallum and Peacock, Centrac, 1992.

2. This notion of community roots was vividly explained by one of my consultees by the phrase: "they can't bugger off".

3. 'Pioneer project inspires others', article in *The Times* feature page about the Community Enterprise Scheme Awards, 9 July 1991.

4. *Taking on the Motorway: North Kensington Amenity Trust 21 Years*, Andrew Duncan, Kensington and Chelsea Community History Group, 1992

5. Duncan, op cit.

6. *Coin Street: there is another way...*, Ian Tuckett, Coin Street Community Builders.

7. Quoted in Tuckett, op cit.

8. *Development Trusts Association Feasibility Study*, Fitzpatrick and Jackson, Spring 1992.

9. The Department of the Environment is an English government department; in Scotland and Wales its areas of interest are administered by the appropriate departments of the Scottish and Welsh Offices.

10. In the late 1970s and early 1980s this field work role was often known as 'animation', recognising the need for some form of external stimulus as well as support to get things moving at local community level.

11. The one Scottish region in which no community enterprise support unit has been established is Borders.

12. The Local Government Unit was a non-teaching section of the Social Studies Department which sponsored a range of research and action projects and

published a series of papers and pamphlets.

13. Craigmillar Festival Enterprises Ltd grew out of the job creation work of the Craigmillar Festival Society and traded as an all trades building company with an ambitious apprenticeship policy. That, and the general toughness of the building industry at the time led to its closure some three years later. The legal structure developed for CFEL served as the blueprint for what was to become the basic Scottish model constitution.

14. In other authorities 'APTs' are known variously as designated or priority areas.

15. Clydebank District Council and Renfrew District Council.

16. *Little Pockets of Hope*, Glen Buchanan, LEAP/LGU, 1983.

17. ...or should it be 'tank thinkers'? - anyway they came from the Policy Unit at Number Ten and one of them has succeeded Mrs Thatcher in her Finchley constituency.

18. The Industrial Common Ownership Movement Ltd (ICOM) is the national federation and support organisation for worker co-operatives in Britain.

19. *Model constitution for a company limited by guarantee and not having a share capital* (together with the 'short form' and Special Provisions), and the *Guide to the Specimen Constitutions*, Community Business Scotland Ltd, 1991 and 1992.

20. There is a serious lack of basic information about the extent and nature of the community enterprise sector throughout the country. Even in Scotland where there has been a good support network for some years, information is patchy, out of date and not capable of much meaningful comparison between regions.

21. BACEN is jointly funded by the Local Authority (using urban programme funds) and British Petroleum.

22. The SSHA was a quango which built and managed significant amounts of public sector housing in Scotland. When Scottish Homes was formed it took over all SSHA houses and has been seeking ways of handing these houses on to other housing management organisations.

23. Information folder of the Shape Group: *Housing and more...*

24. It is interesting to note that one of the keys to the development of the Mondragon group of co-operatives in northern Spain was the existence of the local co-operative savings bank which has been able to use local capital for development and expansion.

Chapter 2

1. Quoted in *British Co-operation*, Arnold Bonner, Co-operative Union, 1961.

2. Bonner, op cit.

3. Bonner, op cit.

4. 'Robert Owen's silent monitor', extract from his autobiography and quoted in a leaflet published by New Lanark Conservation Trust.

5. *A New View of Society and Other Writings*, first essay, Robert Owen, Penguin edition, 1991.

6. Owen, op cit.

7. Owen, op cit.

8. *Report to the County of Lanark*, Robert Owen, Penguin edition.

9. Bonner, op cit.

10. It may be that the Local Employment Trading System (LETS - or 'green dollar schemes' in Australia, New Zealand and Canada) will turn out to be the national equitable labour exchanges of the twenty-first century; see Appendix iii for Lets Link UK.

11. G J Holyoake, quoted in Bonner, op cit.

12. Bonner, op cit.

13. *What We Are and What We Stand For*, Co-operative Bank, 1992

Chapter 3

1. Articles of association paragraph 30, Scott Bader Company Ltd, revised 1971.

2. From 1991 the Highlands and Islands Development Board was amalgamated with the Training Agency to form Highlands and Islands Enterprise. The remit of the former HIDB is now divided between HIE and the Local Enterprise Companies which have been established throughout the Highlands and Islands.

Chapter 4

1. The Community Programme (CP) scheme derived from the Job Creation Programme (JCP) first introduced by the Labour Government in the second half of the 1970s. CP offered the unemployed part-time work of community benefit at a 'rate for the job' wage. Employment Training (ET) which replaced it claimed to be training led rather than work led and replaced rate for the job payment with benefit plus £10, plus travel expenses over £5. Employment Action (EA) which was introduced later offered the opportunity of doing community work projects to the long-term unemployed but on the same 'payment' terms as ET. EA has not been popular and the uptake has not achieved government targets.

2. In North America 'Workfare' has been a scheme which ties continued benefit for the unemployed to doing community work. It is partly the fear that Employment Action might develop into such a scheme that has made it unpopular.

3. Compulsory competitive tendering legislation (CCT) has required public

authorities and in particular local authorities to put increasing amounts and types of services out to competitive tender. The rules state that non-commercial considerations may not enter into the allocation of contracts. This has made it impossible for local councils to favour in any way local community enterprises in areas of high unemployment or to put binding local labour clauses into contracts.

4. The only effective research into the local impact of community enterprise has so far been that commissioned by the Scottish Office and carried out by the Training and Employment Research Unit at Glasgow University (*An Evaluation of Community Business in Scotland*, McGregor, McArthur and Noone, Scottish Office Central Research Paper, February 1988). This research confirmed that community businesses were capable of employing the long-term unemployed from the immediate area in which they were situated.

5. See: *Using Local Labour in Urban Renewal: a good practice guide*, R Macfarlane, BITC, Action for Cities, Manchester City Council, 1992.

6. For a good discussion about some of the pitfalls of the 'contract culture' see: *Contracting Lessons from the US*, Richard Gutch, NCVO publications, 1992.

7. 'Ivanhoe Castle gets a new roof', Martin Wainwright reporting in *The Guardian*, 13 August 1992.

8. I am indebted to Andrew McArthur for this very expressive phrase.

Chapter 5

1. 'Common Purpose' is also the name of a national organisation which brings together groups of people in towns, cities and counties throughout the country in a programme designed to improve networking between key local decison-makers and adminstrators and to increase their common understanding of the area in which they live and work. See Appendix iii.

2. APT: area for priority treatment.

Chapter 6

1. In fact Waverley Housing Management has also set up a landscaping enterprise which contracts both to do their in-house landscape work and tenders for other local jobs. In this way additional employment is being created for local people.

2. See, for example, the Development Agreement prepared by Strathclyde Community Business (June 1990) and the very detailed training schedules insisted on by the credit union movement.

Chapter 8

1. *Little Pockets of Hope*, Glen Buchanan, LEAP/LGU, 1983.

2. *Development Trusts Association Feasibility Study*, Fitzpatrick and Jackson, 1992.

3. *New Sector* issue no 2, May/June 1992. *New Sector* is published as the UK journal for community and co-operative enterprise by a consortium of Community Business Scotland, Industrial Common Ownership Movement and Community Enterprise UK.

4. *Creating Jobs Through Community Enterprise: a proposal*, Ball and Pearce, 1980. (The publication of this pamphlet was made possible by a grant from the Calouste Gulbenkian Foundation.)

5. Tony Worthington is the Member of Parliament for Clydebank and was formally a Strathclyde Regional Councillor and Chairman of Strathclyde Community Business Ltd.

6. Moss Side and Hulme Community Development Trust Ltd: see Appendix iii.

7. See, for example, *Gilding the Ghetto: the state and the poverty experiments*, CDP Inter-project editorial team, 1977 and *The Costs of Industrial Change*, CDP, 1977.

Chapter 9

1. *Future Wealth: a new economics for the 21st century*, James Robertson, Cassell, 1990.

2. See: *Company Community Involvement in the UK*, Ruth I Johns, Ruth I Johns Associates, 1991.

3. Quoted in *Wealth Beyond Measure: an atlas of new economics*, Ekins with Hillman and Hutchinson, Gaia Books, 1992.

4. 'Carey in renewed attack on Government', John Mullin reporting in *The Guardian*.

5. 'Prince tells top bosses profit is not all', Will Hutton reporting in *The Guardian*.

6. The principles, which have been produced by the CERES project (the Coalition for Environmentally Responsible Economies) of the US Social Investment Forum, set forth broad standards for evaluating activities by corporations that directly or indirectly impact the earth's biosphere.

7. The Community Re-investment Act 1977 required financial institutions to reveal where they invest their funds and obliged them to help meet the credit needs of the local communities in which they are chartered.

8. The purpose of the *New Consumer* magazine is "to provide people with information and practical strategies for integrating their economic choices with their values and lifestyle": see Appendix iii.

9. 'How the west was not quite won', Michael Meacher writing in *The Guardian*, 10 December 1991.

10. *Whose Business is Business?*, Community Business Ventures Unit, Calouste Gulbenkian Foundation, 1981.

11. *CB News* was the journal of Community Business Scotland which published 44 quarterly issues between December 1981 and December 1991. It was succeeded by the *New Sector* magazine.

12. In Scotland, Scottish Business in the Community.

13. Reported in *The Last LEAP Year: final report of the Local Enterprise Advisory Project*, Paisley College, 1984.

Chapter 10

1. *Investing in Community Enterprise: synthesis of a programme of discussions, consultations and research*, unpublished report, CEI Consultants for Business in the Community, February 1992.

2. ICOF, SCEIF and Mercury are all members of the UK Social Investment Forum (UKSIF) which acts as a networking and information exchange mechanism: see Appendix iii.

Chapter 11

1. It is likely that the Charities Commission or the new Scottish Charities Office might well take steps to prevent obvious abuses of this nature.

2. For example, the Inland Revenue required some years ago that all community business companies in Scotland insert the word "poor" before residents in the main objective clause of their memorandum of association defining the people for whose benefit the company had been established. This necessitated the passing of special resolutions to change the memorandum in order to comply.

3. In Scotland, the Assistant Registrar for Scotland.

4. Articles 139 and 140 of the *Model constitution for a company limited by guarantee and not having a share capital*, Community Business Scotland, 1991.

5. "Current grant on community business development projects will not extend to wages for the main workforce, though key supervisory and managerial positions may be supported, as well as some overheads. The period of such support will be decided on the merits of individual projects. Such projects will be required not to prejudice any existing local business and retention of income will be subject to conditions that the grant should not be used to subsidise unrealistically high (wage) payments to those producing the goods or services; or artificially low costs for services/overheads/rent; or artificially low prices for goods or services offered. In addition, no individual should stand to make a personal gain akin to profit", Urban Renewal Unit, Scottish Development Department, October 1982.

6. The UK Co-operative Council was formed after the winding-up of the National Co-operative Development Agency as a means of maintaining

collective networking and lobbying within the co-operative movement: see Appendix iii.

7. See *New Sector* issue no 3, September 1992.

Chapter 12

1. 'Thinking globally - acting locally', paper given by Hazel Henderson to the second Working for Common Wealth conference held at Christchurch, New Zealand, July 1990.

2. As in: *Investing in Community Enterprise*, CEI Consultants for BITC, unpublished report, 1992.

3. 'Economic conventions: health versus wealth', Dr Peter Draper, *Royal Society of Health Journal*, 1977.

4. Manfred Max Neef quoted in 'Thinking globally - acting locally', Hazel Henderson, op cit.

5. See: *Alternative Economic Indicators*, Victor Anderson, Routledge, 1991.

6. The British government's attempt in the latter part of 1992 to push through the rapid closure of 31 coal mines is a particularly 'good' recent example.

7. The work has been carried out by students on a project from the MBA course at the University of Nottingham and has been organised by the Notts Co-operative Development Agency with consultancy advice from Community Enterprise Consultancy and Research: see Appendix iii.

8. Reported in *New Consumer* issue no 12, September 1992.

Chapter 13

1. See: *A New World Order: grassroots movements for global change*, Paul Ekins, Routledge, 1992.

2. The Basic Income Research Group was formed in 1984 to research all aspects of reform along the lines of basic income and produces regular reports and information sheets: see Appendix iii.

3. Enterprise Rehearsal permitted ET trainees who were researching a self-employment idea to begin to trade while still trainees and in receipt of income, their initial earnings being held 'in trust' until they became fully self-employed and no longer in receipt of benefit.

4. This is funded by Middlesbrough Borough Council and the East Middlesbrough City Challenge and is being implemented by Initiative Management North East Ltd: see Appendix iii.

5. *An Evaluation of Community Business in Scotland*, McGregor, McArthur and Noone, Scottish Office Central Research Unit Paper, 1988.

6. McGregor et al, op cit.

Appendix i

A global context of poverty, ecological threat and human disempowerment

"No arrangement, proceeding from a defined intention to attain an object of desire, could be worse devised than that which is now in practice throughout all the nations of the earth. Immense, invaluable energies, competent with ease to procure everything beneficial to humanity, lie waste, or are so misdirected as to defeat the object of all their wishes."

In the fading years of the twentieth century two major issues face the world as immense problems. The first is the extent of poverty amongst the population and the second is the very health of the eco-systems which sustain life on the planet.

Poverty

Statistics are difficult and poverty is relative to where you are and what you are used to. The *Oxfam News* of autumn 1991 estimated that "throughout the world 1.2 billion people are unable to afford the basic necessities of life...": that is absolute poverty, poverty which effectively cannot sustain life. That is the poverty which we see in harrowing pictures on our television sets. *Oxfam News* continued: "...while the rich countries, with 25% of the world's population, consume 80% of the world's resources. The gap between rich and poor is growing. During the 1980s average income in the UK rose by 20%. In Africa and in parts of Latin America average incomes fell by between 10% and 25%".

The absolute poor are for the most part to be found in the countries of the Third World: the developing nations, referred to collectively as 'the South' in the North-South debate. The relatively poor are mostly to be found in the richer nations where the gap between rich and poor has steadily widened over the past two decades. In the US the top 1% of the population experienced an 85% rise in their real incomes during the 1980s while the incomes of the bottom 20% fell by 12%.[1] *The Guardian* newspaper reported on 16 July 1992 that official figures showed that in Britain "in 1988/9 12 million people were living below half-average income, the nearest thing to an official poverty line"

1. 'Taking the yellow brick road to ruin', Will Hutton in The Guardian.

143

and "that 25% of all children were living below this line in 1988/9 compared with 10% in 1979, indicating that almost 3.2 million children are in poverty".

Threat to the environment

The threat to our environment is many faceted: the global warming due to the emission of greenhouse gases; the depletion of the ozone layer; the pollution of the seas and inland waterways; the continuing deforestation, in particular the depletion of the tropical rain forest; the production and discharge of toxic wastes, the potential impact of which we are too often woefully ignorant; the steady extinction of animal and plant species.

The consequences of the continuing degradation of the planet and exploitation of natural resources which are not renewable are well documented and, during 1992 prior to the Earth summit in Rio de Janeiro, were well publicised. Quite simply it is unsustainable for the world's population to continue exploiting our globe as we have done and do. Sir Shridath Ramphal, former Commonwealth Secretary General, describes what we must do as "the war for human survival...is unlike other wars. It is not a matter of winners and losers. Everyone must lose so everyone may win. Only to the extent that individual nations accept limits and thresholds can there be collective victory. It is not a war of man against man, nation against nation, but rather a war of humanity against unsustainable living. It is the only war we can afford."[2]

The context within which any discussion about development takes place is one in which world-wide poverty is increasing and the planet on which we depend for life itself is being unsustainably damaged. That context affects us all: it is as relevant to development decisions in Britain as it is to development decisions in Bombay. Four other key factors add to this context.

First, is the very fact that we must see the globe as one place. No longer are other countries far distant: what happens on the other side of the world affects us just as deeply as what happens in our own country - indeed sometimes more so. Think of Chernobyl, think of the impact on our weather of the Phillipine volcanic eruption, think of the effect of the hole in the ozone layer, think of the Iraqi invasion of Kuwait, think of Japanese decisions to invest or not to invest. Never has a truism been so accurate: the world is indeed a small place.

Second, the world's population is expected to rise by 97 million people a year for the next decade: the fastest ever rate of population growth. The impact of such growth on the world's resources will be phenomenal as well as the resultant pollution created by the additional consumption of more people. Ninety per cent of the new births will be in poor countries.[3]

2. Earth, a Guardian *publication in association with Oxfam to mark the Earth Summit in Rio, June 1992.*

3. *see* Earth, *op cit.*

Third, throughout the world ordinary people find themselves disempowered: unable to have any impact on the political or economic processes which determine their condition. In many countries this is because there is not even the semblance of democracy but even the so-called democracies are more characterised by unenthusiastic voters who do not believe their vote will exert much influence.

Fourth, despite the ending of the East-West nuclear arms race, arms production and usage is at an all-time high. The arms industry is a key component of the economy of most western states, selling those arms to the growing number of poorer nations engaged in bitter local wars. The break-up of the Soviet Union has resulted in more nations now being nuclear military forces with others around the world probably on the point of developing the technology.

These global problems are awesome and international gatherings of nations and of interests need to address them at the global level. But for any solutions to be effective they must happen at the local level because for most people it is their local reality and their immediate problems which count. Gandhi's dictum "think global, act local" remains relevant. We must try and understand the problems globally and agree frameworks for solutions globally, but action must come at the local level. It is clear that we shall all have to learn to do things differently, and for that very reason we must try to understand how the development of community enterprise in Britain may relate to tackling a set of global problems.

Exploitation

The contrast between North and South, between rich and poor in the world is striking. Twenty-five per cent of the world's population in the richer countries consumes 80% of the energy and controls 86% of world industry. Indeed five nations alone control 60% of industry. The poorest fifth of nations together have 1% of world trade while the richest fifth have 81.2% .[4]

A commodity produced in a typical South country might be sold by the producer for 50 pence and will leave the country of production at a price of, say, £1.00. By the time it is processed and eventually reaches the consumer in a North country the price might be £10.00. Ninety per cent of the value added will have accrued to the Northern economy. This is a continuation of the resource and human exploitation of the colonial era and before, an exploitation vividly explained in an obituary notice for Hammer de Roburt, the first president of Nauru, who died in July 1992: "Since 1907 Australian agriculture had benefited enormously from the availability of cheap Nauran phosphate. The Naurans were paid very limited compensation, despite the steady destruction of their island".[5]

In June the International Court of Justice found in favour of Nauru that

4. see Earth, *op cit.*
5. *'Courageous father of his people', obituary in* The Guardian *28 July 1992.*

Australia had a moral and legal obligation to rehabilitate areas mined. For the most part however the Northern economies flourish off the back of the resources extracted from the South and off development projects which are more concerned about ensuring a proper 'rate of return' on investment than on benefiting the local community. Kavaljit Singh describes the impact of the development by multi-national hotel chains of 35 luxury resorts on the Goan coast-line: "The high-rise hotels are springing up as close to the water front as they wish. The effects on the coastal ecology are disastrous. With each luxury hotel needing at least 30,000 litres of water each day to fill their swimming pool, the wells of the locals in the coastal villages are running dry. The sinking of numerous tube wells on the coast threatens the ingress of saline water to fresh water wells. The destruction of sand dunes has made the coastal villages vulnerable to cyclonic storms. Coconuts and local shrubs have been destroyed and replaced by exotic plants, alien to coastal environment".[6]

Debt and return on investment

During the 1980s billions of dollars were lent to the South countries for the purpose of development projects, leading to the debt crisis affecting both the Northern banks and the Southern nations now that it is apparent that repayment for many is quite impossible. Such is the way of international finance though that rich nations will expect to pay 4% interest on foreign debt while the poor nations are charged 17%. A consequence is that there is a net annual outflow of funds from South to North of some 50 billion dollars. In other words wealth is being drained from the poor to the rich. The worth of aid programmes is less than the payment due on debt.

Conventional thinking with regard to Third World development is dominated by two main notions. First, that any investment must be on sound financial grounds (this despite the records of poor investments at home and abroad which is currently embarrassing the banking world) in that it gives a proper 'return on investment' and second, that development is synonymous with economic growth. With the collapse of eastern block Soviet communism the G7 nations appear to believe that capitalism 'won' the cold war and that capitalism is therefore the 'right' way of running the world economy. What they do not seem to understand is that it is the capitalist way which has presided and continues to preside over a world in which poverty is increasing and where the environmental dangers to survival are frightening.

Seeking an adequate return on investment from projects located in the South may seem to be normal from the point of view of multi-national corporations and international finance; after all their business is to make profits. But it ignores the moral imperative that the North should be transferring to the South the necessary means for reducing the North-South divide rather than increasing it. Similarly economic growth implies that the planet can sustain continued and

6. *'Structural adjustment: who really pays?'*, *Kavaljit Singh*, *Public Interest Research Group, Delhi 1992.*

unlimited resource depletion, increased pollution, species extinction, deforestation, desertification etc. It also implies that the benefits of growth will trickle down to benefit the poorest. In fact the opposite appears to be the case. Instead of benefits trickling down ('cascade' should be what we seek[7]) they seem to accrue to the richer rather than the poorer both between nations and within nations.

The growth illusion

Richard Douthwaite has recently challenged the conventional wisdom that growth is beneficial and argued that in fact in recent decades the negative effects of growth have outweighed the positive. His book, *The Growth Illusion*, is sub-titled "How economic growth has enriched the few, impoverished the many, and endangered the planet".[8] In it he suggests that the pursuit of growth has led to rising unemployment, to worsening crime rates, to poorer standards of health and education, to less contentment with life, to turning rural Third World subsisters into urban slum-dwellers, and of course to the steady and continuing degradation of the planet.

The rich are unfairly using the resources of the world to their exclusive advantage. That must end and the implication of ending it is for the richer nations to use their wealth and know-how for the benefit of the whole world and accept the probability of a levelling off of standards and, more especially, of expectations of continued growth. That of course is exactly what President Bush refused to accept when in the run-up to the Rio conference he expressed his concern that decisions at the conference might limit the US "to a course of action that could dramatically impede long-term economic growth in this country".[9]

Rich and poor

"Two nations; between whom there is no intercourse and no sympathy; who are as ignorant of each other's habits, thoughts, and feelings, as if they were dwellers in different zones, or inhabitants of different planets; who are formed by a different breeding, are ordered by different manners, and are not governed by the same laws."[10]

The problem is not just between rich and poor nations. It exists within all nations. In Britain and in the US, for example, the disparity between rich and poor has worsened in the past two decades. The poverty of the rundown

7. Soon after his unexpected re-election in April 1992 Prime Minister John Major spoke about his wish for created wealth to "cascade" down the generations.

8. The Growth Illusion, Richard Douthwaite, Green Books, 1992.

9. 'Bush not keen to attend Earth Summit', report in the Malaysian New Staits Times, *23 April 1992.*

10. Sybil or The Two Nations, a novel by Benjamin Disraeli, first published 1845; Penguin edition 1980.

housing estates on the edges of our great cities contrasts vividly with the wealthy suburbs and the business class hotels. Arriving at Bombay's international airport with its runways lined by some of the world's poorest shanty town dwellers and travelling down-town to the richest tourist and business area is a similar and unforgettable experience. The rich and powerful the world over are part of an international network. It is not essentially a problem of North against South, G7 against the rest, rich nations against the poor nations: the problems affect us all. It is more international capital against mankind; the economy as god with the mass of humanity sacrificed to keeping it in good humour. The problems and issues facing the poor, the ordinary people, the disadvantaged and the disempowered around the world have much in common.

In his book *The Myth of the Market*, Jeremy Seabrook[11] describes the common problems shared by the people of Easterhouse, Glasgow and Dindoshie, Bombay. The places are very different, but: "The landscapes couldn't be more different: in the monochrome grey of Glasgow's biggest housing scheme, scoured by Atlantic winds, everything is hard and unyielding, stone, concrete, metal, glass. There could be no greater contrast than with Dindoshi: a place of relentless sun, bare red-brown rocks, sparse, thorny vegetation, dust swirling around the uneven self-built structures. At first sight, these might appear to be alien and mutually incomprehensible settlements. Yet both communities bear the same stigmata of those who must live off the fag-end of market economics; and accordingly, there is more to unite than to separate them..."

The August 1992 unemployment figures showed a further significant increase to 2.75m. However after 30 changes to the definition of unemployment since 1979, all but one reducing the number of people who could be designated as unemployed, the figure understates what would have been considered the true scale of unemployment 15 years ago. Most commentators agree that the true figure is now nearer 4 million people. High unemployment has been epidemic in our society for more that two decades and is now endemic. It has grown fastest and highest in those local areas already suffering from lack of work. It has been exacerbated by industrial re-structuring, 'shake-outs'; 'down-sizing': all symptoms of huge changes happening to the world economy which make it probable that there will never again be sufficient jobs to offer 'full employment'.

Where there is high unemployment there is a constellation of other problems all inter-related: poor housing, shoddy environment, indifferent education, lack of public transport, health difficulties. All inter-relate and interact, giving rise to a cycle of deprivation, of depression. These are the communities where it is hard for people to believe they and their families have a future. A police superintendent quoted in *The Guardian* says: "Throughout the area we have this problem of disaffected youth. It's a 'no hope' situation in terms of having no stake in society. Parents are unemployed, maybe grand-parents too. They see all

11. The Myth of the Market: promises and illusions, *Jeremy Seabrook, Green Books, 1990*.

the trappings of a modern society completely beyond their reach".[12]

It is that lack of a stake in society, that alienation which leads to the disaffection demonstrated so vividly by civic unrest. What happens on British housing estates is modest compared, for example, to the disturbances in Los Angeles and to the slums of Bombay but the roots are the same: unfairness, a sense of no future, and the abject failure of the present systems to provide for all mankind.

People-centred development

The Commonwealth Association for Local Action and Economic Development (Commact) was founded at a conference held in Goa, India in 1988 on the notion that the poor and disadvantaged throughout the world face common problems. The first conference of 75 local activists and development workers quickly discovered a common bond and produced a joint statement emphasising the importance of people-centred development. That statement was revised at the third conference held in 1992 in Malaysia and the full text of the new 'visions statement' is reproduced in a later appendix. The central paragraph states: "Commact believes that truly people-centred development will use the human, natural, technological and financial resources of the world for the well-being of the whole of humanity".

That is the essence of an alternative view of the way the world's economy should be oriented: that the purpose of development should be to improve the well-being of all people and to do it without degrading the planet. That is a very different imperative from those which drive the world economic and financial machine.

One of the best definitions of people-centred development is to be found in a paper presented by Sue Dahn of the Victorian Women's Trust to the third Working for Common Wealth conference.[13] She writes: "When we talk about people-centred development, we are talking about a concept that embraces not the business development, not the economic activity, not the large-scale housing, transport or recreational developments or any other large or small-scale projects in and of themselves or for their own sakes alone. What we are talking about could be any or all of these activities or other activities altogether, that have as their objectives benefits, results and outcomes, both short and long-term, that are people-centred, that improve the position of our communities and the people in them.

"People-centred developers are interested in analysing the value of a development not in terms of its effect on the developer's profits, not in terms of

12. 'The urban horror on our doorstep', report by Peter Hetherington in The Guardian.

13. 'Innovations in financing people-centred development', paper presented to the third Working for Common Wealth conference by Sue Dahn, Victorian Women's Trust, Australia, April 1992.

its effect on the national accounts and not in terms of its effect on the industry or business sector, but in terms of what it can do for our countries, our communities and our people.

"People-centred developers want to talk not just about what is being developed, but about why it is being developed (what and whose needs it will fulfil - the developer's or the community's?), about how it is to be developed (what resources will it use?, will the community make an input into the planning of the development?, will local capital be used?, will local labour and skill be used?, what will be the effect on the natural environment?) and who is involved in the development? (who will own and use and who will share in the fruits of the development?).

"People-centred developers care about the outcomes, the results and the impacts of the development rather than the development itself. Can it last over time? What will it take from and what will it give back to our community?"

People-centred development is the 'big idea' which the community enterprise movement in Britain, along with other groupings, agencies and organisations in Britain and around the world, is promoting as an alternative to the conventional wisdom. It is an idea which is based on important principles, but which is essentially practical. It is an idea which depends on local action, but within a global context.

In his book, *A New World Order: grassroots movements for global change*, Paul Ekins chronicles the endeavours of many people who are at the forefront of this alternative thinking and doing.[14] It is stimulating to read about tireless campaigns for human rights, for international security based on peace and nuclear-free weaponry, for wise environmental projects, and about community-based savings and loan schemes, self-build housing projects, local factories making safe, appropriate and affordable medicines, consumer co-operatives, community and co-operative enterprises: all examples of development which is people-centred, people-led and sustainable; and predicated on a value base of co-operation and mutual aid rather than competition.

Notwithstanding all the inspiration demonstrating what can be and, therefore, what might be, the task ahead is huge. It is hard to see how the sum total of all the disconnected schemes, campaigns and projects which Ekins describes can add up to the sort of global force needed to stop the prevailing political and economic thinking in its tracks and turn it around. Indeed it seems rather that world power is vested in fewer and fewer hands and is effectively beyond the political control even of nation states. Ekins concedes that the "grassroots movement for global change" is a fragile task force: "The organisation of this people's power into a force that can both resist the big

14. A New World Order: grassroots movements for global change, *Paul Ekins, Routledge, 1992.*

battalions and further the common good is a formidable and uncertain task".
Yet that is the task force of which the community enterprise movement is a
part.

Appendix ii

List of consultees

1. Sir Kenneth Alexander; one-time Chairman of the Highlands and Islands Development Board, initiator of the Community Co-operative Scheme.

2. Colin Ball; Chair of Commact, founder of the Centre for Employment Initiatives.

3. George Burt; former Director of Community Business Scotland, Chair of Waverley Housing Management Services.

4. Martin Caldwell; Regeneration Consultant, former Glasgow District Councillor.

5. Pat Cassidy; Manager of Govan Workspace Ltd.

6. Mike Gahagan; Department of the Environment.

7. David Grayson; Business in the Community.

8. Richard Gutch; Arthritis Care, formerly National Council of Voluntary Organisations.

9. Keith Hayton; University of Strathclyde Department of Planning.

10. Robin Heal; Community Affairs Adviser to British Petroleum.

11. Paul Henderson; Community Development Foundation.

12. Martin Hilland; Regeneration Consultant, former Manager of the Woodlands Community Development Trust Ltd and Glasgow District Councillor.

13. George Hood; Convenor of Community Business Scotland, Tayside Regional Councillor.

14. Margaret Jackson; Eldonian Development Trust.

15. Tor Justad; Community Enterprise Support Unit (Central Region) Ltd.

16. Alan Kay; Community Enterprise Lothian Ltd.

17. Peter Kuenstler; CEI Consultants.

18. Andrew McArthur; Training and Employment Research Unit, University of Glasgow.

19. Roger Matland; North Kensington Amenity Trust Ltd.

20. Amobi Modu; Finsbury Park Development Trust Ltd.

21. Roy Pederson; Social Development, Highlands and Islands Enterprise.

22. John Popham; Chairman of Community Enterprise UK.

23. James Robertson; author of *Future Work* and of *Future Wealth*.

24. David Robinson; Community Links Newham.

25. William Roe; CEI Consultants, former Convenor of Community Business Scotland and Chair of Craigmillar Festival Enterprises Ltd.

26. Colin Roxburgh; Community Enterprise Consultant, former Senior Development Worker with Strathclyde Community Business Ltd.

27. Peter Smith; University of Durham, one-time of Sunderlandia Ltd.

28. Ian Tuckett; Coin Street Community Builders Ltd.

29. Alan Tuffs; West Calder Community Holdings Ltd.

30. Mike Walker; The Allander Group Glasgow, Vice-Convenor of Community Business Scotland.

31. John Watt; Highlands and Islands Enterprise, formerly Social Development, Highlands and Islands Development Board.

32. Tony Worthington; Member of Parliament, former Strathclyde Regional Councillor and Chairman of Strathclyde Community Business Ltd.

Appendix iii

Directory of organisations referred to in the text

Action Resource Centre
First Floor
Park Village East
London NW1 3SP
tel: 071 383 2200

The Allander Group
Possil Community Business Ltd
136 Strathmore Road
High Possil
Glasgow G22 7DW
tel: 041 336 3141

Association of British Credit Unions Ltd
Unit 307
Westminster Business Square
399 Kennington Lane
London SE11 5QY
tel: 071 582 2626

Association of Community Enterprises in the Highlands and Islands
103 High Street
Invergordon
Ross-shire IV18 0AB
tel: 0349 853500

Association of Scottish Development Organisations
c/o Solway Community Business
49 Buccleuch Street
Dumfries DG1 2AB
tel: 0387 50793

Basic Income Research Group
102 Pepys Road
London SE14 5SG
tel: 071 639 9838

Bootstrap Enterprises
The Print House
18 Ashwin Street
London E8 3DL
tel: 071 254 0775

Bristol and Avon Community Enterprise Network
Hebron House
Slon Road
Bedminster
Bristol BS3 3BD
tel: 0272 637634

Business in the Community
227A City Road
London EC1V 1LX
tel: 071 253 3716

Calouste Gulbenkian Foundation
98 Portland Place
London W1N 4ET
tel: 071 636 5313

Capital Strategies
23 Hampstead Road
Birmingham B19 1BX
tel: 021 515 1956

Central Govan Housing Association
35 McKechnie Street
Govan
Glasgow G51 3AQ
tel: 041 440 0308

Civic Trust Regeneration Unit
17 Carlton House Terrace
London SW1Y 5AW
tel: 071 930 0914

Co-Enterprise
138 Digbeth
Birmingham B5 6DR
tel: 021 643 4343

Coin Street Community Builders
99 Upper Ground
London SE1 9PP
tel: 071 620 0544

Common Purpose
12 - 18 Hoxton Street
London N1 6NG
tel: 071 729 5979

Commonwealth Association for Local Action and Economic Development (Commact)
Commact House
PO Box 11779
50756 Kuala Lumpur
Malaysia
tel: (03) 2550977

Commact Europe
c/o Community and Youth Course
Department of Adult and Continuing Education
University of Durham
32 Old Elvet
Durham DH1 3HN
tel: 091 374 3733

Community Business in the North East
65 Beatty Avenue
Jesmond
Newcastle upon Tyne NE2 3QS
tel: 091 285 7679

Community Business Scotland
Society Place
West Calder
West Lothian EH55 8EA
tel: 0506 871370

Community Enterprise Midlands
100 Lyttleton Street
West Bromwich
West Midlands B70 2SB
tel: 021 569 2157

Community Enterprise UK
100 Lyttleton Street
West Bromwich
West Midland B70 2SB
tel: 021 622 2747

Community Enterprise Wales
Community Activities Centre
Godreaman Street
Aberdare
Mid Glamorgan
tel: 0685 877150

The Co-operative Bank plc
1 Balloon Street
Manchester M60 4EP
tel: 061 832 3456

Development Trusts' Association
c/o North Kensington Amenity Trust
1 Thorpe Close
London W10 5XL
tel: 081 969 7511

East Middlesbrough Community Venture Ltd
Beresford Buildings
The Greenway
Thorntree
Middlesbrough
Cleveland TS3 9MB
tel: 0642 230 314

Eldonian Development Trust
Tony McGann Centre
7 Eldonian Way
The Eldonian Village
Liverpool L3 6JL
tel: 051 207 3406

Finsbury Park Community Trust
259/261 Seven Sisters Road
London N4 2DD
tel: 071 263 3138

Govan Workspace Ltd
Elderpark Workspace
100 Elderpark Street
Govan
Glasgow G51 3TR
tel: 041 445 2340

Helmsdale Heritage Society
Timespan Heritage Centre
Bridgend
Helmsdale
Sutherland KW8 6RH
tel: 0431 2327

Industrial Common Ownership Finance Ltd
12 - 14 Gold Street
Northampton NN1 1RS
tel: 0604 37563

Industrial Common Ownership Movement
Vassalli House
20 Central Road
Leeds LS1 6DE
tel: 0532 461738

Initiative Management North East Ltd
Southlands Centre
Ormesby Road
Middlesbrough
Cleveland TS8 0HB
tel: 0642 327583 x 263

Islay and Jura Pool Enterprises Ltd
Coille
Gruinart
Bridgend
Islay
Argyll PA44 7TT
tel: 0496 81205

John Lewis Partnership
171 Victoria Street
London SW1E 5NN
tel: 071 828 1000

Langridge Crescent Housing Co-operative
Langridge Initiative Centre
Langridge Crescent
Berwick Hills
Middlesbrough
Cleveland TS3 7LU
tel: 0642 249148

Leicester City Council
New Walk Centre
Welford Place
Leicester LE1 6ZG
tel: 0533 549922

LETS Link UK
61 Woodcock Road
Warminster
Wiltshire BA12 9DH
tel: 0985 217871

Loftus Development Trust
The Council Offices
25 High Street
Loftus
Saltburn
East Cleveland TS13 4HA
tel: 0287 641342

Mercury Provident plc
Orlingbury House
Lewes Road
Forest Row
Sussex RH18 5AA
tel: 034282 3739

Middlesbrough Borough Council
Vancouver House
Gurney Street
Middlesbrough
Cleveland TS1 1QP
tel: 0642 221029

**Moss Side and Hulme Community
Development Trust**
11 Parisian Way
Moss Side District Centre
Moss Side
Manchester M15 9NQ
tel: 061 226 8705

**National Federation of Credit
Unions**
Credit Union House
102 Tong Street
Bradford BD4 6HD
tel: 0274 687 692

**National Federation of City Farms
AMF House**
93 Whitby Road
Brislington
Bristol BS4 3QF
tel: 0272 719109

**National Federation of Housing
Associations**
175 Gray's Inn Road
London WC1X 8UP
tel: 071 278 6571

New Consumer
52 Elswick Road
Newcastle upon Tyne NE4 6JH
tel: 091 272 1148

The New Economics Foundation
Universal House
Second Floor
88 - 94 Wentworth Street
London E1 7SA
tel: 071 377 5696

New Sector **Magazine**
Unit 44
West Calder Workspace
Society Place
West Calder
West Lothian EH55 8RE
tel: 0506 871370

North Kensington Amenity Trust
1 Thorpe Close
London W10 5XL
tel: 081 969 7511

**Nottinghamshire Co-operative
Development Agency**
Dunkirk Street
Dunkirk
Nottingham NG7 2PH
tel: 0602 705700

Papay Community Co-operative
Beltane House
Papa Westray
Orkney KW17 2BU
tel: 08574 267

People for Action
44 Bradford Street
Birmingham B5 6HX
tel: 021 622 2747

**Queens Cross Housing
Association**
840 Garscube Road
Glasgow G20 7ET
tel: 041 945 3003

Scott Bader Commonwealth
Wollaston
Wellingborough
Northamptonshire NN9 7RL
tel: 0933 663100

**Scottish Business in the
Community**
Romano House
43 Station Road
Corstorphine
Edinburgh EH12 7AF
tel: 031 334 9876

Scottish Community Enterprise
Investment Fund plc
West Calder Workspace
Society Place
West Calder
West Lothian EH55 8EA
tel: 0506 871370

Scottish Federation of Housing Associations
(including the Confederation of
Scottish Housing Co-operatives)
5 Park Terrace
Glasgow G3 6BY
tel: 041 332 8113

The Shape Group
44 Bradford Street
Birmingham B5 6HX
tel: 021 622 2747

Shared Interest Society Ltd
52 Elswick Road
Newcastle upon Tyne NE4 6JH
tel: 091 272 4979

South London Family Housing Association
Rochester House
2 Belvedere Road
London SE19 2HL
tel: 081 653 8833

Start-up
9 Broadway
Salford M5 2TS
tel: 061 872 3838

The Stroud Pound
The Old Convent
Beeches Green
Stroud
Glos GL5 4AD
tel: 0453 757 411

Traidcraft plc
Kingsway
Gateshead
Tyne and Wear NE11 0NE
tel: 091 491 0591

UK Co-operative Council
PO Box 101
1 Balloon Street
Manchester M60 4PT
tel: 061 829 5290

UK Social Investment Forum
Vassalli House
20 Central Road
Leeds LS1 6DE
tel: 0532 342080

Waverley Housing Trust
27 North Bridge Street
Hawick TD9 9BD
tel: 0450 77797

Welsh Development Agency
Community Enterprise Unit
Business Centre
Triangle Business Park
Pentrebach
Merther Tydfil CF48 4YB
tel: 0685 722177

Welsh Federation of Housing Associations
Norbury House
Norbury Road
Fairwater
Cardiff CF5 3AF
tel: 0222 555022

West Calder Community Holdings Limited
West Calder Workspace
Society Place
West Calder
West Lothian EH55 8RE
tel: 0506 871222

Appendix iv

Selected bibliography

An Evaluation of Community Business in Scotland, McGregor, McArthur and Noone, Scottish Office, 1988.

Alternative Economic Indicators, Victor Anderson, Routledge, 1991.

A New View of Society and Other Writings, Robert Owen, Penguin edition, 1991.

A New World Order: grassroots movements for global change, Paul Ekins, Routledge, 1992.

Bootstrap: ten years of enterprise initiatives, Martin McEnery, Calouste Gulbenkian Foundation, 1989.

British Co-operation, Arnold Bonner, Co-operative Union, 1961.

Community Business: good practice in urban regeneration, DOE, HMSO, 1990.

Community Enterprise in the Local Economy, ed McGregor and McArthur, TERU Research paper series, University of Glasgow, 1990.

Community Trading Organisations: a review of community enterprise characteristics and practices, Currie, McCallum and Peacock, Centrac, 1992.

Company Community Involvement in the UK, Ruth Johns, Ruth I Johns Associates, 1991.

Contracting lessons from the US, Richard Gutch, NCVO publications, 1992.

Creating Development Trusts: good practice in urban regeneration, DOE, HMSO, 1988.

Future Wealth: a new economics for the 21st century, James Robertson, Cassell, 1990.

Future Work, James Robertson, Temple Smith/Gower, 1985.

Guide to the Specimen Constitutions, Alexander Stone and Co for Community Business Scotland, 1992 (to be used in conjunction with the specimen constitutions, 1991 edition).

Little Pockets of Hope, Glen Buchanan, Local Enterprise Advisory Project, 1983.

Putting People First, Godric Bader, the Scott Bader Commonwealth, 1990.

Redefining Wealth and Progress: new ways to measure economic, social and environmental change; the Caracas Report on alternative development indicators, Bootstrap Press, 1990.

Signposts to Community Economic Development, ed Paul Henderson, Community Development Foundation, 1991.

Small is Beautiful: a study of economics as if people mattered, E F Schumacher, 1973.

Taking on the Motorway: North Kensington Amenity Trust 21 years, Andrew Duncan, Kensington and Chelsea History Group, 1992.

The First Ten Years: a decade of community enterprise in Scotland, Community Business Scotland with the Association of Community Enterprises in the Highlands and Islands, 1988.

The Growth Illusion, Richard Douthwaite, Green Books, 1992.

Towards a New Sector: macro policies for community enterprise, New Economics Foundation, 1992.

Using Local Labour in Urban Renewal: a good practice guide, Richard Macfarlane, BITC, 1992.

Wealth Beyond Measure: an atlas of new economics, Paul Ekins, Gaia, 1992.

Appendix v

Three definitions of community enterprise

1. A Community Business is a sustainable commercial enterprise which is owned and controlled by the local community. It aims to create jobs and related training opportunities and to encourage local economic activity. Profits are used to create more jobs and businesses and to generate wealth for the benefit of the community.

Usual characteristics

a. A community enterprise is a business which aims to create sustainable jobs and related training activities for local people and/or provide commercial services.

b. A community enterprise aims to make profits and to become financially self-sustaining and to use profits for re-investment in the enterprise, for limited bonus payments to workers and to generate wealth for the benefit of the community.

c. Membership or share-holding in the community enterprise is organised on democratic one-person one-vote principles.

d. A community enterprise must be registered either as a company or as a co-operative society using a model or other legal structure which is recognised as acceptable by Community Business Scotland or by the Association of Community Enterprises in the Highlands and Islands.

e. The assets of the community enterprise are owned on behalf of the community and held in trust by the directors such that the assets may not be disposed of to benefit individual members or directors financially.

f. The membership of the community enterprise must be open to all persons within its agreed area of benefit. In some circumstances a 'community of interest' or a 'community of need' can be established.

g. The community enterprise is committed to being a good employer regarding wage levels, terms and conditions, equal opportunities and employee participation.

h. The community enterprise should be encouraged to evaluate and report on the effectiveness of its impact on the local community.

Community Business Scotland
December 1991

2. A Community Enterprise is an organisation which aims to encourage local economic activity and which:

- exists for the benefit of a defined community based upon geography or other common interest;

- is principally owned and controlled by the members of that community;

- aims to deliver local opportunities for jobs, training, a more active economy, a better infrastructure or just an improved environment;

- seeks to become financially self-sustaining and make a surplus which is primarily re-invested in the enterprise or is used for the benefit of that community.

Business in the Community
Investing in Community Enterprise
February 1992

3. Development Trusts differ widely in their nature and format but in general they are:

● independent and aiming for self-sufficiency;

● not-for-private-profit;

● community-based but with differing degrees of community control;

● a partnership between the community, voluntary, private and public sectors;

● engaged in the economic, environmental and social renewal of a defined area or community;

● often companies limited by guarantee and sometimes with charitable status.

Development Trusts have community benefit at the heart of their concern.

Development Trusts Association Feasibility Study
Spring 1992

Appendix vi

Commact Visions statement 1992

C·O·M·M·A·C·T

Commonwealth Association
for Local Action and Economic Development

c/o 22. JALAN SETIAJAYA, DAMANSARA HEIGHTS, 50490 KUALA LUMPUR, MALAYSIA.
P.O. BOX 11779. 50756 KUALA LUMPUR, MALAYSIA.
TEL: 03-2550977 FAX: (03) 2549995

The COMMACT Vision and Actions:

We are living in a world where control of financial, technological, natural and human resources is in great measure invested in dominant financial, commercial, industrial and military institutions, both corporate and state.

COMMACT is an organisation committed to people-centred development.

Its members are people working in Commonwealth and other countries in and with organisations in the non-governmental, voluntary, public, private and grass-roots sectors.

The work and concerns of these organisations span the whole spectrum of development needs: economic, social, political, cultural, educational and environmental.

COMMACT believes that truly people-centred development will use the human, natural, technological and financial resources of the world for the well-being of the whole of humanity.

People-centred development is a continuing process designed to transform existing power relationships by empowering people, their organisations and their communities at local, regional, national and international levels. Such transfer of power to people and communities will enable them to control the decisions and actions which affect their lives. As a consequence, the decision making powers and processes of existing institutions will be changed. By fostering self-reliance and social/economic independence, people-centred development aims to increase individual, collective and community self worth, dignity and security.

Recognising the diverse and changing needs of all minority, special needs and indigenous groups, COMMACT's policies and programmes are committed to achieving real equality for these groups. Moreover, COMMACT will endeavour to ensure that governments acknowledge these needs in the implementation of developing policies and in legislative structures. In particular, COMMACT recognises the central role of women in all forms of people-centred development.

Neither state socialism nor the free market system has cared enough for the outcomes of development in terms of people and the natural environment. They neither promote nor enable people-centre development, but rather had led to under-development, wrong development, ecological disaster, social disintegration, and the alienation of whole groups within society.

Development can only be effective through strengthened local action. For example:

* by enhancing local human resources through locally devised training;

* by promoting local decision making on issues of local improvement;

* by enabling and assisting people to establish local agencies to affect this; such as credit unions, local development organisations and enterprises which contribute to the economic well-being of marginalised communities.

* by creating alternative policies and institutions to effect the transformation of existing power structures so that they become based on the principle of democratic management and accountability at local, regional, national and international levels.

Furthermore, all these policies and practices should take full account of the need to respect and enhance cultural and environmental conditions.

COMMACT will promote its visions by:

* exchanging information about the impact of global forces on local action, and the reverse;

* lobbying and advocacy at appropriate levels;
* undertaking research, promoting training and education and facilitating the provision of technical assistance;

* empowering people to formulate and implement their own policies;

* promoting understanding of social issues at all levels.

In particular COMMACT will:

* continue to publish case studies on all forms of people-centred development and to publish its regular newsletter, COMMactions;

* publicise particular examples of local empowerment to broaden understanding of the process and practice of people-centred development;

* continue with the task of establishing and promoting its Technical Assistance Fund and Network;

* promote and assist the COMMACT Indigenous Women's Network through information and personnel exchange;

* promote and strengthen its regional groupings and associations;

* establish working parties to examine its membership structure and arrangements and its international and regional structures.